A GAIJIN'S GUIDE TO
JAPAN

Also by Ben Stevens
*From Lee to Li: An A–Z Guide of
Martial Arts Heroes*

A GAIJIN'S GUIDE TO
JAPAN

An alternative look at Japanese
life, history and culture

Ben Stevens

The Friday Project
An imprint of HarperCollins Publishers
77–85 Fulham Palace Road
Hammersmith, London W6 8JB
www.thefridayproject.co.uk
www.harpercollins.co.uk

First published by The Friday Project in 2009

A catalogue record for this book
is available from the British Library

ISBN 978-1-906321-21-5

Designed and typeset by Maggie Dana
Illustrations by Jorge Santillan

Printed and bound in Great Britain by
Clays Ltd, St Ives plc

Mixed Sources
Product group from well-managed
forests and other controlled sources
www.fsc.org Cert no. SW-COC-1806
© 1996 Forest Stewardship Council
FSC

FSC is a non-profit international organisation established to promote
the responsible management of the world's forests. Products carrying
the FSC label are independently certified to assure consumers that
they come from forests that are managed to meet the social, economic and ecological needs of present or future generations.

Find out more about HarperCollins and the environment at
www.harpercollins.co.uk/green

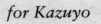

for Kazuyo

INTRODUCTION

In 1853, a Reverend Samuel Wells Williams – in Japan to act as translator to Commodore Matthew Perry (*See* **Black Ships, The**) – declared the Land of the Rising Sun to be '… the most lewd of all the heathen nations I have seen'.

As it transpired, however, the good Reverend was a bit of a dork who couldn't even speak Japanese all that well, so we shouldn't take his opinion too seriously. He was merely distressed that women laboured bare-breasted in the paddy fields – a fact which, if he'd lightened up a little, may well have actually put a smile on the miserable old coot's face.

Since then, a host of academics and other experts on Japanese history, language, culture and customs have pondered such important questions as: Why did nearly every Japanese woman under the age of thirty go nuts over **David Beckham** during and after the 2002 World Cup? Why will saying '**Chin-chin!**' at a Japanese drinking party result only in stony stares and an awkward silence? And is it *really* true that many *samurai* warriors liked – in their spare time – to get 'down and dirty' with one another?

Here, finally, are explanations concerning these and many other weighty matters. (Around 200 of them, in fact.) I have compiled this book while residing in Japan, teaching English for a living (surprise, surprise), immersing myself in *judo* and *karate* training (the *origami* course was full) and occasionally indulging in the mystical, ancient art of *karaoke*.

In *A Gaijin's Guide* ..., I set out to record everything that struck me as being relevant to this fascinating country. You hold the end result in your hands. Hopefully it will entertain, enlighten and otherwise delight you. Now, *hajimashou* – let's begin ...

A

ABE, SADA

I can pretty much guarantee that any male reading this is shortly going to be crossing his legs and wincing ... You ready? Okay – born in 1905 to a respectable family of *tatami* makers, Sada Abe became a rebellious teenager whom her parents, in despair, sold to a *geisha* house. Unwilling to undertake the years of rigorous training necessary to become a *geisha*, however, Abe became a prostitute instead.

She seems to have had an insatiable appetite for sex, indulging in a string of lovers, as well as paying customers. However her physical desire came at a cost: on several occasions throughout her life, she would require treatment for syphilis.

It was when Abe quit prostitution to become a waitress that she met the man whom she thought would become the love of her life. Kichizo Ishida was the (married) owner of the Yoshidaya restaurant in Tokyo where Abe worked, and the pair were soon embroiled in an affair. His sexual stamina left even Abe reeling; on occasion the pair remained in bed for anything up to four days, with Ishida sometimes demanding that a *shamisen* player perform for them as they made love.

When Ishida rejected her for a time and returned to his wife, Abe was devastated. They briefly resumed their affair – this time experimenting with 'erotic' asphyxiation (they tightened an *obi* or 'belt' around each other's neck at the moment of climax) – but Abe was paranoid that Ishida would leave her again.

Early on the morning of May 18, 1936, Abe strangled Ishida to death (using their treasured *obi*) as he slept. Then, using a knife, she hacked off his penis and testicles before depositing them – wrapped in newspaper – in her handbag. (Kind of makes the old bunny-boiling routine all seem a bit tame, really.) Using the blood to write 'Sada and Kitchi together' on the bed-sheets, Abe then went on the run, managing to evade the police for three days before being captured (by which time the 'Abe Sada Incident' had successfully scandalized the whole of Japan). She told the police: '... I knew if I killed him, no woman would ever touch him again.'

At the resulting trial – and contrary to her own wishes, as well as those of the prosecution – Abe was not given the death penalty. She instead received a mere six years for the murder of her lover and the subsequent mutilation of his corpse. (The luckless Ishida's genitalia, meanwhile, were put on public display for a time at Tokyo University's Medical School. Nothing like letting the poor sod rest in peace, was there')

Ultimately, Abe served only five years' imprisonment, being released in May 1941. She attempted to resume her life under an alias, and again had a succession of lovers – but each time the relationship ended when her real identity inevitably became known. (Can't think why ...) In the end, Abe accepted a curious form of employment, being paid to appear at a succession of inns, to cause the male patrons to experience a pleasurable frisson of fear as she stared haughtily at them.

Later in her life, Abe largely disappeared from public view, and it's not known exactly when she died. But it's believed to have been some time around 1987, when Abe would have been aged approximately eighty-two – for only then did she finally stop putting flowers on Kichizo Ishida's *haka* (tomb).

The 'Abe Sada Incident' was the inspiration for the sexually explicit (of course) 1976 movie, *In the Realm of the Senses*.

AINU

Comparisons between the *Ainu* and the native Indians of North America abound, although the Japanese wouldn't thank you for saying so. According to *Ainu* legend, they were in Japan '100 000 years before the Children of the Sun' – but as soon those 100 000 years were up, they began losing territory to the Japanese pretty darn steadily.

The *Ainu* resided mainly to the north of the country, particularly on the island of Hokkaido, which would eventually become their final place of refuge. Their story is depressingly familiar the world over: bullied and hounded from anywhere the Japanese wanted for themselves; forced to agree to unfair land-share deals that were then broken anyway, and brutally dealt with on the few occasions when they tried – always unsuccessfully – to meet force with force.

For a while, the *Ainu* were left in relative peace in Hokkaido, although following the **Meiji Restoration** the large and sparsely populated island began to be viewed as the perfect solution to what, in the rest of Japan, was fast becoming an overcrowding problem.

More and more Japanese began to move to Hokkaido. In case they should be disturbed by the indigenous population – who if they were male didn't shave once they'd entered adulthood, and who if they were female commonly had a variety of facial and body tattoos – the Meiji 'government' (in truth more like an oligarchy) outlawed the *Ainu* language and many of their customs, while forcing them to live on state-owned 'farming plots'.

Today, an estimated 150 000 *Ainu* remain, although many choose to keep their identity a secret due to the discrimination they continue to suffer. Their language is also threatened with extinction: there are well under 1 000 native speakers left.

AKACHOCHIN

The closest thing Japan has to a Western-style public house, the *akachochin* is readily identifiable by the large red lanterns hanging outside. (*Akachochin* literally means 'red lantern' – in days gone by these signified that somewhere sold alcohol.)

Just open the sliding door and venture inside, and if you can't make head nor tail of the food menu that's usually written entirely in Japanese, it probably doesn't matter. There'll often be at least one customer who speaks sufficient English to help you decipher the à la carte menu, or you can just gesture – with a polite and very Japanese-like movement of the hand – at something you see being eaten that looks quite tasty.

Perhaps you fancy some *yakitori* (pieces of chicken and onion barbecued on skewers) or maybe you're willing to try grilled squid. And to go with it – beer or *sake*? The choice, as they say, is yours.

AKANAME

Commonly used by parents to scare children into cleaning the bath, an *akaname* (a combination of two words: *aka* or 'dead skin', and *name*, which comes from the verb *nameru* – 'to lick') is a human-cum-frog-like creature with wild hair, an incredibly long tongue and a single clawed toe. It has a penchant for entering dirty bathrooms in the dead of night and licking them clean, which would be very nice of it, if its left-over saliva did not subsequently cause an illness in any human who came into contact with it. And by 'illness' I don't mean a nasty rash or a touch of flu. No, the *akaname* is frequently credited with causing such serious maladies as pneumonia and cancer. Which is, if you ask me, a bit much, even to scare the most unruly of children into cleaning the bathtub.

B

BASEBALL

In Japan, it's popular. Real popular. Just like football in England, for many it's more like a way of life. Amateur adult teams across the country meet up at some ungodly hour in the morning to practise before work. Two middle-aged women to whom I teach English, have previously requested to end a lesson early so that they could get back home to watch a particular game. Every high school has a number of young men whose dream is to be the next 'Godzilla' – otherwise known as Hideki Matsui, the craggy-faced batter and pitcher, who now (following a nine-year spell with the Yomiuri Giants) plays for the New York Yankees.

It was an American, Horace Wilson – working in Japan as a Professor of English at what is now Tokyo University – who introduced the game of baseball to the Land of the Rising Sun. Sometime in 1872/73, he organised a team to play during the students' lunch-break. Baseball's popularity consequently spread like wildfire – and, for his efforts, Wilson was inducted into the 'Japanese Baseball Hall of Fame' in 2003, some seventy-six years after his death.

BECKHAM, DAVID

He was mobbed everywhere he went! Japanese boys and young men wore their red Manchester United shirts with pride as they bellowed their adoration! Some female office workers even styled their hair into a bleached blond Mohican in tribute!

And then David Beckham allegedly had an affair and lost it all. Such a loss of face is serious stuff in Japan, and the resulting public disgrace and humiliation (which will, of course, only occur if you're famous) can last years.

You might stand half a chance of regaining the lime-light if you wait a suitable length of time before grovel-ling for forgiveness, but, let's face it, Becks had basically cleaned up by then anyway. When I was in Japan in 2003/2004, there seemed to be scarcely a product – from cars and phones, right down to bars of candy – that he wasn't being paid squillions of yen to advertise.

Strangely enough, Posh was quick to jump on the bandwagon, hence the slightly vomit-inducing advertisement for a 'his-n-hers' perfume that featured a head-and-shoulders snap of her and Becks together, the single word underneath – *Beauty*.

It all depends on your personal definition of the word, I suppose.

BENKEI

One of Japan's best-loved folk heroes, Benkei was either the supernatural offspring of a **temple** god or the son of a blacksmith's daughter, depending on which story you believe.

In any case, he came kicking and screaming into this world with hair and teeth already in place. A natural troublemaker, he soon earned the nickname *oniwaka* or 'young devil child', which to be honest probably just made him act up even more. In spite of this misbehaviour, he was trained as a monk, and by the age of seventeen stood a two-metre tall giant with the strength of a small bull.

'I've had enough of living in stupid Buddhist monasteries,' he said at this point, in a teenager's surly grunt. 'I'm going to go and hang out with the *yamabushi* [mountain priests who were quite handy at fighting] who sound way cooler.'

Suitably trained in martial arts and warfare – and particularly expert in his use of the sword – Benkei then decided to place himself by Gojo Bridge in Kyoto, where he set himself the target of beating 1 000 thousand men using his sword.

Rather unsurprisingly, 999 men were beaten without any problem whatsoever. It was that very last man who proved a bit of a tricky bugger. Along he sauntered, playing a jaunty tune on his flute, a little sword flapping at his side.

'Hah! I'll easily best this pipsqueak,' gloated Benkei.

'Hey!' he called as the small, slightly built man drew closer. 'If you want to cross this bridge with all your limbs intact, just you hand over that sword! Otherwise it will be the worst for you, see?'

'You big oaf,' laughed the slightly built man. 'My name is Minamoto no Yoshitsune, son of the infamous warlord Minamoto no Yoshitomo. If you don't get out of my way right this second, I'll thrash you like the insolent dog you are.'

'Oh, I just love it when I get a wise guy,' declared Benkei, his eyes betraying a feral light as he rushed towards his intended victim.

Stepping nimbly out of the way, Yoshitsune then used his flute to hit the giant sharply around the head. Benkei let out a roar and flashed his great sword all around him – but each time, Yoshitsune was simply not there. This battle required such little effort on Yoshitsune's behalf that he was frequently able to play a little tune on his flute (he was undoubtedly a bit of a smartarse, but then having a famous warlord dad can do that to you).

Finally, exhausted with cutting through nothing but thin air – and really wishing that Yoshitsune would stop playing that same bloody tune – Benkei slumped to the ground and conceded defeat.

'Okay, you win,' he told Yoshitsune. 'Here – I demanded your sword, so it's only right that you should now have mine.'

But Yoshitsune only laughed, probably played his flute a bit more, and then sat down beside the fallen giant. He explained that he'd been trained in martial arts and swordsmanship by the *tengu* (mythological creatures), which meant that he only ever needed to draw his sword in times of extreme peril.

'No offence, Benkei,' he said, patting the much larger man on one of his ox-like shoulders, 'but you're all mouth and no trousers.'

At which Benkei apparently begged to become Yoshitsune's loyal follower, for however long they both should live.

So off they went and had lots of adventures, until it all turned a bit nasty and Yoshitsune found himself being betrayed by his powerful brother. Holed up in Takadachi Castle, an entire army just about to force their way inside, Yoshitsune killed first his family and then himself, to prevent them from falling into enemy hands. Benkei, loyal to the last, remained outside the room where his fallen master lay, defending it until his great body was finally brought down by over one hundred arrows.

A rather dubious postscript is occasionally added to this story, which entails four or five people walking along a remote track a few days later, their features concealed under rough brown cloaks.

'Phew,' says one of the group, casting off his cloak to reveal a small sword and a flute by his waist. 'I think we're far enough away from the castle now, boys and girls.'

'What a good job you found some people who looked uncommonly like you, me and your family, master!' declares another, far larger man.

'Even more fortunate that they didn't mine dying for us.'

'Rather!' say Yoshitsune's family (the members of which remain somewhat anonymous), as they all head towards the sanctuary of a forest above which hangs the slowly setting sun.

BLACK SHIPS, THE

In 1853, Japan was a country largely closed to the world. The foreign policy of the ruling Tokugawa Shogunate was *sakoku* – 'closed country' – and had been since 1639.

The only real exception to the rule that prevented the Japanese from leaving Japan, and the **gaijin** from entering, on pain of death, was in Nagasaki. Here there was *Dejima*, an artificial island that was the official trading post for the Dutch; Holland being one of four countries, along with Korea, China and the Ryukyu Islands, with whom the Tokugawa Shogunate consented to trade.

From 1837, three separate attempts were made by the Americans to 'open up' Japan trade-wise, both to themselves and, by implication, to the rest of the world. Effectively, the Americans were demanding that Japan put an end to its long period of self-imposed isolation.

'Not on your Nelly,' returned the Tokugawa Shogunate (or words to that effect), on a number of occasions actually opening fire on their unwelcome visitors.

Finally the Americans decided that they were gonna kick some 'A', or at least threaten to. Step forward Commodore Thomas Perry, who, in charge of a fearsome-looking squadron of steam frigates (this was the nineteenth century, remember), set sail from Norfolk, Virginia, reaching Uraga Harbour near Edo (now Tokyo) on 8 July 1853.

Slightly in awe of the steam-driven fleet's obvious firepower, the Tokugawa Shogunate politely asked Perry if he wouldn't mind sailing along to Nagasaki, which was, after all, the only place where *gaijin* sailing vessels were permitted to dock.

'Actually, I would mind,' said Perry, presumably through a translator. 'I'm here to present a letter from President Fillmore of the United States of America, requesting that Japan ends its period of isolation,'

And by obvious implication, he added: *And if you don't accept this letter and at least start to consider the*

*request – which is actually more like a direct order
from the most powerful nation on earth – then I'm
going to use those nasty-looking cannons onboard my
ships to start blasting the crud out of you.*

'Oh dear ...' muttered the Tokugawa Shogunate del-
egates.

'As and when my boats and I return from a trip to
China,' continued Perry, 'you'd be well advised to have
a positive response to that letter.'

Perry wasn't to be disappointed. When the black-
hulled ships returned the following year, belching omi-
nous clouds of smoke, the Tokugawa Shogunate signed
a treaty committing it to 'relations' with the USA. This
marked the beginning of the end for the feudalistic
Shogunate, who would finally be overthrown by the
Meiji Restoration in 1868.

BON

Commonly called *Obon* (the 'O' is honorific, as in
okane – 'money'), this is the Buddhist 'Festival for the
Dead', which occurs from 13 – 15 July in the east of
Japan (where the Western solar calendar is favoured)
and the same dates in August in western parts of the
country (where the Chinese lunar calendar is still
followed).

You'll see the countless sprawling cemeteries within
Japan full of people cleaning the family *haka* (a Buddhist tomb) and paying their respects to the spirits of

their ancestors, who return to earth on the thirteenth of either month for a total of three days.

During this time, the spirits generally fly around and look in on their loved ones, who as well as cleaning the family *haka* may also hang lanterns outside their homes by way of welcome.

BONSAI

In the film *The Karate Kid*, Daniel LaRusso first comes to know Mr Miyagi through helping him tend his many *bonsai*. As *bonsai* require constant care and attention, Mr Miyagi would have needed all the help he could get. In fact, with that many *bonsai* to look after, it's doubtful that Mr Miyagi would have been able to hold down his job as a handyman, never mind teach young Danny boy the finer points of Japanese fisticuffs.

One of the things *The Karate Kid* doesn't teach you – or maybe it does; it's been a long time since I've seen it – is that *bonsai* first came to Japan from China, where they'd been around since the days of the Tang Dynasty (that's a long time, believe me).

Controversy amongst *bonsai* aficionados continues to rage as to whether Chinese *bonsai* were merely trees already dwarfed by nature, thus making the Japanese the first people who were able to stunt a normal, healthy tree so that it can grow only between twenty-five centimetres to one metre tall.

Of course, you can't just stick a young sapling in a pot and expect it to flourish. Because it wouldn't; it would die. No, what you must do is to continually prune the fledgling *bonsai*, carefully removing every excess branch and twig until you've created the image you want for it. Perhaps you'd like it to resemble a wind-gnarled tree that's situated on the very edge of a seaside cliff – your choice.

With sufficient care and attention – including frequent re-potting, root pruning and fertilisation – *bonsai* can last hundreds of years, passed down through generations. Though I suspect that the one Mr Miyagi gave Daniel's mum probably ended up in the bin about a week later.

BOWING

'Oh boy – anything to do with Japanese etiquette is an absolute minefield ...'

So runs the usual reply from someone claiming to be expert on all things Japanese, in response to a question concerning when to bow, how to bow, and so on. In reality, if you get an answer like this then the person speaking probably doesn't know too much themselves – or is just trying to scare you.

Certainly, Japanese etiquette can be incredibly complicated. But that's something to worry about if you're Japanese, or have lived and worked in Japan long enough for it to become an issue. And even then, quite often it won't become an issue, simply because, whether you like it or not, you're a *gaijin* who's presumed not to know too much about such matters.

Smile – but not too broadly – when you meet someone (excessive smiling can be an indication of unease in Japan, and can also make you look a bit weird), and for the purpose of this exercise give something like a 'half-bow' from the waist. Don't just nod, because that looks a bit half-arsed in any country. If you're male, keep your hands by your waist; females should put their hands on their thighs with their fingers touching.

When saying goodbye, another bow can be given, though not as deep as the first one. And that's about it. I've given the information about where to put your hands as general guidance, though to be honest the fact that you're prepared to give any sort of bow will be appreciated by most Japanese people.

Oh, and by the way, it may well be that some Japanese people will offer to shake hands. It's not true that the Japanese never shake hands; I've shaken hands with numerous Japanese men, as well as several women (albeit in a business environment). But let the person you are meeting offer their hand first – if they don't, stick with the bow.

One final piece of advice: don't ever try to embrace or kiss someone upon meeting them, even if it's for the fourth or fifth time and you think that you're getting on just fine. It might just result in you being branded a *chikan* and arrested.

BUDDHISM

Obviously anything like a detailed account of Buddhism is not going to be supplied here. All I can do is to provide the briefest overview, as the Japanese perceive it.

Around 623 BC, a baby boy was born to the king of a tribe who existed on the Indian border of present-day Nepal. Siddhārtha Gautama, as the boy was named, was destined for a life of great luxury and indolence, his father determined that he should never be exposed to human suffering. At sixteen, Gautama married his cousin, and all in all spent twenty-nine years of his life stuck behind the walls of his father's palace.

Then one day he grew so sick of his cosseted, uneventful existence that he ventured outside the palace. And what he saw shook him to the core: there was Old Age (an elderly man), Illness (a leper or someone with an obvious disease), Death (a decaying corpse) and – spot the odd one out – an ascetic.

Gautama was profoundly depressed by three of these sights, and so decided that the only way to defeat Old Age, Illness and Death was to follow the ascetic's example and become a monk, disowning his inheritance and trying to understand how he could overcome suffering through meditation.

And meditate he did, on his own and with other hermits and monks; but still this didn't give him satisfaction. So off he roamed around India, where he decided to try and gain 'Enlightenment' through depriving himself of all creature comforts, including food.

After nearly perishing of starvation, Gautama decided that starving himself wasn't really such a good idea. He instead chose what Buddhist's refer to as the 'Middle Way': neither over-indulging nor denying himself something to the extent that this denial became physically harmful. Aged thirty-five, Gautama decided to sit beneath a bo tree, and not stand back up until he'd achieved Enlightenment. Which, to cut a long story short, is eventually what happened.

Ignorance was the principal course of human suffering, he realised, and he had the Four Noble Truths (which are really a bit too deep to go into here) or 'steps' that anyone could follow to defeat ignorance and thus become Enlightened.

To bring this story to a rather abrupt conclusion, Buddha (as he was now known) spent the last forty-five years of his life travelling extensively and gaining many followers. He died aged eighty, having fallen ill after eating a meal of what is commonly believed to have been pork. Exercising true benevolence, however, he refused to blame the man (named Cunda, a blacksmith) who'd given him the meat dish.

'All composite things pass away. Strive for your own salvation with diligence,' were Buddha's final words before dying.

What's important to point out here is that Buddha

didn't claim to be any sort of god. Nor was he unique; he was merely the last in a long line of people who could also be called Buddha, people who'd also gained Enlightenment. In fact, according to my brother-in-law Taigi, who is the Buddhist head-priest of a temple belonging to the *Jodo* – 'Pure Land' – sect of Buddhism, there are (and this is a direct quote, including the pluralising of the word 'Buddha') '... as many Buddhas as there are grains of sand in this world ...'

I suppose it just so happens that because he was the last of all these trillions of 'Buddhas', the Buddha who was previously Siddhārtha Gautama is the one getting all the attention. In other words, it's been rather a long time since anyone new became a Buddha.

Failing to gain Enlightenment, humans are instead endlessly reincarnated, moving among the Six Realms that are *Ten* (basically heaven, which can't be all bad), *Ningen* (which is the world as we know it, Jim), *Chikusho* (inhabited by animals), *Shura* (described by Taigi as being filled with an 'everlasting anger'), *Gaki* (where you suffer from a general dissatisfaction and want of everything) and, finally, *Jigoku* (hell).

One of these days, then, someone will succeed in gaining Enlightenment and will thus break this vicious circle, thereby creating a new Buddha. In the meantime, Buddhists do their best to stay out of the 'lower' Realms by filling their lives with selfless acts of charity.

BUDŌ

The 'umbrella' term given to all types of Japanese martial arts. *Budō* itself is a compound of two Japanese words: *bu* meaning 'war', and *dō* meaning 'way of'. *Budō* best describes the myriad fighting skills a *samurai* warrior would have needed to master in order to survive the battlefield. He (not many female *samurai* in feudal Japan, though check the *Naginata* entry for the inevitable exception) would have been highly skilled in not only archery and swordsmanship – from which come *kendō* and *iaidō* – but also in striking and grappling.

Hence the martial art *jujutsu* (there are various spellings of this word, but my Japanese laptop recognises only this one, so that's the one I'll use), which was born on the battlefields of ancient Japan. *Jujutsu* was then – and sometimes still is today, depending on where, and from whom, you learn it – a comprehensive fighting system, with the violent, 'anything goes' philosophy that you'd expect from a martial art that was learned very much 'on the job'.

BURAKUMIN

In a country that remains as obsessed with a person's 'roots' and family history as Japan, coming from *burakumin* stock can still cause someone some serious prejudice. The word itself means 'people of the hamlet' – which is a nice way of saying that feudal-era *buraku-*

min were confined to an almost ghetto-like existence, forbidden to associate with non-*burakumin* to the extent that they were even required to have their own **temples** and shrines, so that they should live as isolated a life as possible.

In fact, *burakumin* were commonly known then as *eta*, or 'full of filth', and endured pretty much the same existence as the 'untouchable' class in India. They did the sort of jobs that were wholly necessary yet at the same time were considered unclean – think undertaking, tanning, and really anything that involved dead flesh and bodies – all the while being informed by **Shinto** priests that they were contaminating themselves with the impurities created by death. In fact, for sheer revulsion, their occupations were ranked equal to the crimes of bestiality and incest. Hence the reason why they were forbidden to associate with anyone of a 'higher' position than themselves in the feudal caste system – and they were right down there at the bottom.

Anything between 1 – 3 000 000 *burakumin* descendants live in Japan today, some (like the **Ainu**) doing their best to disguise their background, while others continue to live in the – mainly rural – areas where *burakumin* have traditionally had their 'hamlets'.

BUSHIDŌ

Or 'Way of the Warrior' (literally 'Warrior's Way', though that doesn't sound half as good), encompasses the typical 'manly' characteristics, such as self-control, perseverance, courage, honesty, loyalty and so on.

Inazo Nitobe, in his famous book imaginatively entitled *Bushidō* (it would probably have to be called *Fighting Techniques of Japan's Deadly Flying Samurai Ninja Warrior Monks of Death* to succeed in today's market) observed that the *samurai*'s code of practice wasn't that different from the Western knight's chivalric code, and most fighting forces dating from the beginning of time would probably claim to possess the above attributes.

Bushidō expected the *samurai* to readily meet his own death at a moment's notice – a death he was often required to mete out to himself through the act of *seppuku*, or the cutting open of his own belly with a short sword. This was thought to release the *samurai*'s spirit in the most dramatic way possible (I'd have to agree with that), and was the only way to escape defeat on the battlefield or to avoid some other source of great shame.

Naturally, *seppuku* was extremely painful. Hence the usual presence of another *samurai*, armed with a long sword with which to cut off his friend's head and end his suffering the moment the act was completed.

BUSHUSURU

On January 8, 1992, at a state dinner given in his honour during a visit to Japan, President George Bush

Snr. repaid the hospitality of his hosts by throwing up in the lap of Prime Minister Kiichi Miyazawa. The unfortunate incident was quickly blamed on a feeling of 'nausea' that had plagued Bush all that day; but soon the verb *Bushusuru* – literally, 'doing a Bush' – had been invented to describe those who vomited without warning.

BUSH WARBLER, JAPANESE

You're much more likely to hear rather than see this little critter, though to be honest you won't be missing all that much. The Japanese Bush Warbler, or *uguisu*, is usually small, brown (sometimes with a hint of dark yellow around its belly) and ... er ... that's about it really.

The beauty of its mating call – which I won't even attempt to transcribe here – commences from around the start of spring, and once led to it being dubbed 'the Japanese Nightingale'. This name, however, completely ignored one important point: namely, that the *uguisu* never chirps away at night.

This bird also lends its name to that special type of *ninja*-defeating flooring, *uguisubari*. It's also often mentioned in *haiku*, given its association with spring, *sakura*, and other things that tend to get the Japanese excited. And if that's still not enough, an enzyme found in its droppings is used both as a skin-whitening agent and to remove stains from a *kimono*.

BYŌBU

Folding screens that originally came from China, *byōbu* ('wind wall') could at first be found only in the Emperor's court. *Byōbu* acted as draught excluders (hence the name), room sub-dividers and in general livened the place up a bit with the colourful pictures of dragons, mountains, lakes, great trees and the like that were painted upon them.

Around the fifteenth century, however, *byōbu* had become so commonplace that nearly everyone – rich and poor – owned at least a couple. Hence their fall from favour: *byōbu* are nowadays commonly seen gathering dust inside **temples** and museums, dragged out every now and then for such occasions as weddings.

C

CHIKAMATSU, MONZAEMON

Renowned seventeenth century playwright, whose enduring fame has often led to him being referred to as the 'Japanese Shakespeare'. The son of an unemployed doctor, he began his career writing *haiku*, before really making a name for himself by knocking out well over 100 plays. Few of these plays, however, are what you might call cheery. In fact, with titles such as *The Love Suicides at Sonezaki* and *The Love Suicides at Amijima*, the audience knew that they were going to be watching something a tad 'deep'.

Later in his career, Chikamatsu transferred his formidable talents to *bunraku*, or the 'puppet theatre', where frequently just one person would chant the lines for any number of puppet 'actors', all the while accompanied by a lone *shamisen*. Sound a little more cheery? Don't you believe it. Chikamatsu was a man obsessed:

suicide (and death in general) in his plays – for puppets or otherwise – remained a common theme.

CHIKAN

Means 'molester' or pervert. Commonly refers to disturbed males taking advantage of packed Toyo commuter trains to grope whichever female is squashed up nearest to them. But sexual assaults of this nature are just as likely to occur at rock concerts and in crowded shopping malls. There are even signs by some bicycle parking lots, warning women to be on their guard as they bend down to undo their bicycle locks.

At the time of writing, an economist named Kazuhide Uekusa (formerly a well-known TV commentator) has been indicted by public prosecutors in Tokyo for allegedly molesting a female high school student on a train in September 2006.

If found guilty, it will be Uekusa's second offence: he was convicted in 2004 of using a handheld mirror to look up a schoolgirl's skirt while the pair of them were stood on an escalator. Fined ¥500 000, his career and reputation in ruins, he was also ordered to surrender his precious mirror, net worth ¥100 (about fifty pence).

You'd have thought that would have taught him – I mean, those ¥100 mirrors must surely mount up – but here's Uekusa, apparently back to his old tricks. Despite having only 'hazy memories' of the whole incident, due to his earlier consumption of twenty cups of

Chinese wine, Uekusa vigorously denies this latest charge.

'My hand touched the student when the train rattled,' he's been quoted as saying, 'and I may have been misunderstood.'

To which the majority of the Japanese population reply: 'You certainly are misunderstood, wacko-boy.'

However, the nature of his defence does raise a serious point. Namely that on some trains during certain times of the day – and especially during the Tokyo morning and evening rush-hours – people are packed together so tightly that it is impossible not to have some sort of physical contact with the person next to you.

Chikan have commonly relied on this fact to disguise their nasty deeds, and are assisted by the traditional reluctance of Japanese women to cause a scene, even if they suspect they are being assaulted. But times are changing. Kazuhide Uekusa himself was captured after the female student he was allegedly groping shouted 'Stop! Stop!' and then – assisted by other commuters – performed a citizen's arrest on him.

But there is a growing, discomforting feeling that many men have met a similar fate through what has been a genuine accident. Take, for example, Hideki Kato, who whilst on a packed train was grabbed, apparently at random, by the man next to him when a thirteen-year-old began to scream that she'd been groped.

The Japanese legal system has an unfortunate habit of presuming guilt, and commonly favours those who confess (an expression of sincere remorse by a murderer often helps them avoid the death penalty, and may even result in a reduced prison sentence). So many men accused of being *chikan* feel that they have no choice but to pay the fine, if they wish to avoid going to prison.

Not so Hideki Kato, who stubbornly proclaimed his innocence in court, only to end up receiving an eighteen-month jail sentence. He continues to fight back through the 'Victims of False Accusations Network', although in a few similar cases the accused male has ended up committing suicide.

Many trains now have carriages adorned with pink lines and signs stating that they are *Josei Sennyō Sharyō*: 'For Women Only'. Hopefully this will reduce the number of women being assaulted – and also the number of men who are undoubtedly being falsely accused of being *chikan*.

CHIKATETSU SARIN JIKEN (SUBWAY SARIN INCIDENT)

On the morning of 20 March, 1995, at around 7.30 a.m., five men boarded trains at various stations along the Tokyo subway system and dropped a couple of small, polythene packages upon the floor. Inside these packages was the deadly nerve agent sarin – a pinhead-sized drop of which is more than enough to kill an adult.

Piercing these packages with a couple of jabs from an umbrella, the five men then hastened off the train, each meeting with a 'getaway driver' at a pre-arranged spot. One man called Kenichi Hirose, however, was not quite quick enough – beginning to feel the effects of sarin poisoning, he was obliged to inject himself with the antidote each of the men carried.

The five men – along with their getaway drivers – belonged to the *Aum Shinrikyo*, a shadowy religious cult whose leader was the fat, partially sighted son of a *tatami* mat maker. This man, Shoko Asahara, lusted after a violent coup that would topple the government from power and install him as emperor – deciding that this was something of a tall order, however, he instead elected to unleash a poison on the 5 000 000-plus civilians who use the subway system every day.

Twelve people died in the attacks, and close to a thousand were injured – one woman so seriously that she later lost both her eyes. Asahara and his followers' lunacy deeply distressed a country that had, until then, considered itself to be virtually free of crime – at least of the violent variety.

At the time of writing, Shoko Asahara remains on death row, sentenced to hang. Three of the ten men who carried out his orders – poisoners and getaway drivers – remain at large.

'CHIN-CHIN'

So, you're there at an *akachochin* and are having a whale of a time with your Japanese friends. You've probably figured out by now that *kanpai* means 'cheers' but, after saying it numerous times – while also teaching your social circle its English equivalent – you begin to wonder how else you can initiate another round of beer-glugging.

'I know,' you think, brain just a little fogged with Kirin lager and lovely warm *sake*, 'I'll say "chin-chin" instead!'

Don't. Because plenty of *gaijin* before you have had to learn the hard way – through an awkward silence and shocked stares from their Japanese companions – that "chin-chin" is, in the Land of the Rising Sun, slang for 'penis'?

CHŌMEI, KAMO NO

Famed writer, monk and hermit, born around 1155. His father was a *Shinto* priest in charge of an important shrine. When his father died, it was naturally assumed that young Kamo would step into his shoes. As it transpired, however, this was not to be.

'Sorry,' said whoever it was who decided such matters, 'but we want someone with a wee bit more experience for this job.'

Deeply disillusioned by this, and grieving still for the

loss of his father, Kamo turned to a priest called Shomyo (who may, in fact, have been the young man's grandfather) for some words of wisdom.

'Concentrate on composing poetry,' was Shomyo's rather obscure advice; and with a shrug of his shoulders and a sigh, this was just what Kamo proceeded to do.

In fact, he had something of a knack for it. Within a few years, he'd had an anthology of some one hundred poems published, with a few finding favour within the imperial court.

Kamo, however, soon considered his emerging fame and fortune to be something of a fickle thing. He was becoming obsessed with the Buddhist concept of *mujō*, or impermanence – the idea that this world, and everything in and of it, from gods to insects, is in a constant state of flux. With this in mind, considered Kamo, what was the use of money and material items?

To the bemusement of everyone around him, Kamo retreated to a group of mountains called Ohara, where he changed his name to Ren'in. A move to another mountain called Toyoma followed, before Ren'in performed his anti-materialistic and wandering-hermit-like masterstroke: determined as he was to live in a sublime state of poverty, renouncing all worldly wants and desires, he built himself a shabby hut that, at exactly ten foot square, was what an estate agent might call 'cosy'.

It was here that Ren'in wrote his masterful essay *Hōjōki* (often translated, with an obvious eye on the bestseller list, as 'An Account of My Hut'). Its opening sentence perfectly defines *mujō* thus: 'Ceaselessly the river flows, and yet the water is never the same ...'

Ren'in saw things through to their logical conclusion, expiring in his hut a few years later.

CREATION MYTH, JAPANESE

Once upon a time, a very long time ago, there was nothing. But then something that was lighter than nothing rose to the top of nothing and formed heaven. (This is, quite honestly, the only way I can think of interpreting the original telling of the *Shinto* creation myth, as related in Japan's oldest chronicle, *Kojiki*.)

The heavier mass of nothing, meanwhile, formed what was to become earth. But for a long while 'earth' was nothing more than a vague, watery substance, from which sprouted 'like reeds' lots and lots of gods. But as this vague and watery place wasn't exactly packed full of things to do, the gods soon became bored.

'Look,' they said to two of their number ('Izanami', a female deity, and 'Izanagi', who was male), 'why don't you both pop up to the Floating Bridge of Heaven, and while you're up there see if you can't somehow form some landmasses down here?'

'And how in the name of *Shinto* are we supposed to do that?' demanded Izanami and Izanagi (or just 'Iza and Iza', on the occasions when they didn't need to be distinguished between).

'We haven't got the foggiest,' replied the other gods, 'but take this bejewelled spear with you, in case it should come in handy.'

So up went Iza and Iza to the Floating Bridge of Heaven, where they gazed down at the foggy, watery void.

'Let's see if we can't stir things up a bit, by using this extremely long spear,' suggested Izanami.

'Okay,' replied Izanagi, doing just that – although he was surprised when the spear touched something solid that lay underneath the vague, watery substance.

'What the ... '' he began in surprise, retracting the spear. As he raised it back up towards the bridge, great drops fell from its points. And lo! Instantly as they hit the foggy, watery substance they formed a solid land-mass – an island.

Iza and Iza went from the Floating Bridge of Heaven to the island they'd formed, and decided that they now quite fancied indulging in a bit of hanky-panky. But in the ensuing courtship ritual, Izanami flattered Izanagi first, which for some reason was something that was strictly forbidden by the gods who dwelt in heaven.

Punishment was dealt to Iza and Iza through the birth of their first child, who was 'boneless like a leech' and otherwise generally unsatisfactory. Thus the unfor-tunate child was put on a tiny raft made out of reeds

and set adrift on the foggy, watery substance that surrounded the island.

A second child (called Awashima, or 'faint island' –
presumably something of an insult) proved just as
repellent as the first, and met a similar fate. In despair,
Iza and Iza went up to heaven to ask the gods what
they could do to make amends.

'Re-enact your courtship ritual, only this time make
sure it is the male who compliments the female first,'
said the gods sternly.

'Understood,' nodded Iza and Iza, muttering under
their breaths, 'Jeez, lighten up ...'

But doing as they were told, they were consequently
blessed with children who proved so satisfactory that
they were able to become Japan's three thousand-odd
islands. In fact, so fertile were Iza and Iza that they also
gave birth to gods of wind, trees, mountains, rivers, sea
– although when it came to giving birth to the god of
fire, it all proved too much for poor old Izanami; the
effort killed her.

D

DAIBUTSU

In 743, Shomu, the forty-fifth Emperor of Japan, ordered an urgent meeting of his most trusted advisors.

'Look,' he told them, 'things can't go on like this. Recently we've had a smallpox epidemic, widespread crop failure, and – stone the crows – even an attempted coup. I'm beginning to get the feeling that someone up there doesn't really like me, you know what I mean?'

One of Shomu's advisors awkwardly cleared his throat.

'If by "someone" you mean Buddha, master, then I have a plan ...' he declared cautiously.

'Oh aye?' yawned Shomu. 'Let's hear it, then.'

As he spoke, the advisor warmed more and more to his idea. 'Why don't we build an absolutely flippin' humungous statue of the Buddha, say around sixteen metres tall, with its fingers alone each the size of a human being? It will use up almost the country's entire

stock of copper, but you wait and see if any more droughts or whatever occur after we've erected that little effort at Todaiji temple in Nara ... master.'

'You mean like a dedication, right?' said Shomu. 'Sounds great – get cracking, lad.'

Nine years later, the statue finally completed, an Indian priest named Bodhisena conducted the 'eye-opening' ceremony in front of some 10 000 people. Since then (and it has been rather a long time) such calamities as **earthquakes** and fires have caused the Daibutsu of Todaiji to have to be rebuilt on several occasions; but – though a little smaller than it was originally – it can still be visited to this very day.

DHARMA DOLLS

Expect to see these in many Japanese homes and businesses, as a general sort of good-luck charm. The doll is a depiction of Bodhidharma, the wandering monk who's often accredited with having started the Chinese *kung-fu* style of fighting, along with establishing *Zen* as a means of attaining Enlightenment (*See* **Buddhism**).

Bodhidharma generally favoured walking as a means of transportation; although on occasion (legend informs us) he chose to float across a river on a single reed. However, after nine years sat facing a cave wall in a state of deep meditation, his legs and arms either atrophied or fell off altogether, depending on what version of the story you choose to believe. In any case, this is the reason why the Dharma doll has no limbs painted upon it. (I can only assume that Bodhidharma introduced *kung-fu* to the world before he suffered such grave injuries.)

Dharma dolls are bought without their eyes having been painted in; the owner is supposed to do this him- or herself – one eye at a time – when a particular wish or desire has been fulfilled.

Bodhidharma is said to have had a particularly piercing stare – caused, no doubt, by the fact that he once amputated his own eyelids in a fit of rage after he fell asleep while meditating. These eyelids fell to earth and from them, believe it or not, sprouted the first tea plants.

DIAZ, CAMERON

Just what does your average Hollywood superstar do when their bank-balance needs topping up? Well, they can always – in the case of Ms Diaz, or indeed Brad Pitt – appear in a Japanese television commercial for a mobile phone company. Such commercials play upon an actor's general image: Diaz hams up her familiar 'kooky' role by awkwardly pushing a loaded supermarket trolley with one hand, advertised mobile firmly clamped to her ear with the other, one high-heeled shoe about to fall off as she walks pigeon-toed while chattering away. Brad Pitt, meanwhile, is strolling through an exquisite garden as he talks into his phone. He passes two attractive women, who distract his attention and with whom he exchanges flirtatious glances. Not looking where he is going, he stumbles into an ankle-high water feature.

Ho ho!

While they are undoubtedly paid ludicrous amounts of money for such commercials (the soundtrack for which, incidentally, is Aerosmith's *Walk This Way*), Ms Diaz and Mr Pitt do seem willing to poke a little fun at themselves. Catherine Zeta-Jones, however, in a commercial for a brand of shampoo (or conditioner, or something) appears to have been transformed into some kind of modern-day Greek goddess: eyes sparkling, lips pouting and black hair dutifully gleaming as she stands upon a floodlit podium with (in near-darkness), a cast of thousands below her, all of them pointing, gasping, taking photos, fawning, fainting, etc.

It's tastefully done, anyway, and doubtless helps sell said product.

DŌJŌ

Traditional training hall for Japanese martial arts. A *dōjō* may have bare wooden floorboards for such martial arts as *karate* or *kendō*, or a special type of *tatami* for *budō* that involve throwing, i.e., *judō* and *aikidō*.

Strictly speaking, a *dōjō* should be cleaned by the lower-grade students either prior to or after the training session, although in all but the strictest *dōjō* that's gone rather out of the window.

It used to be that a student wishing to join a *dōjō* – particularly if its head *sensei* had a particularly good reputation – was permitted to do nothing else except clean the *dōjō* for anything up to a year before they were considered a student and allowed to begin their training.

Unlike some *dōjō* nowadays, then, it wasn't all too common to find lots of fourteen-year-old black belts strutting around.

DŌKYŌ

A Buddhist monk, Dōkyō was present at the Imperial Court in Heijo-kyo (present day Nara) when, in 761, the Empress Koken fell sick and seemed likely to die. Somehow Dōkyō succeeded in curing her, and the grateful Empress subsequently made him her Prime Minister. Soon it was popularly believed that the Empress and the monk were embroiled in an affair; *Dōkyō* himself was rumoured to be extremely well-endowed. (A saying of the time was that '... when Dōkyō sits down, three knees protrude'.)

The monk, however, was getting greedy for more power. In fact, he declared that no less than a **Shinto** god or **kami** had declared that he was to be the next Emperor. Curiously, this seems not to have annoyed the

Empress Koken (or Shōtoku, as she was now known). In any case, Dōkyō continued to live within Nara, enjoying his many privileges and doubtless exercising his third knee on occasion.

But his arrogance had angered many within the Imperial Court – and when Shōtoku died in 770, Dōkyō's enemies were at last able to have their revenge. Dōkyō was banished to a distant part of Japan, where he languished in obscurity for the following two years until his death, aged seventy-two.

DRINK DRIVING

Alcoholism has long been recognised as being almost epidemic within Japan, particularly manifesting itself in drink driving. In fact, in any given week you can almost guarantee that several police officers will be arrested for the offence (and this is an entry that I will, for obvious reasons, leave entirely free of any 'comic' exaggeration).

On television, news reporters can frequently be seen running up to people who are obviously not sober, and demanding to know why they are about to get inside their vehicles. To which the frequent response by the intoxicated driver runs something along the lines of, '*Dakara nani?*' – 'So what?' The near-daily interviews with the relatives of those killed by drunken hit-and-run drivers could tell these halfwits exactly 'what', though, depressingly, no one seems to be taking the slightest bit of notice of those people whose lives have been left shattered.

E

EARTHQUAKES

Over 1 000 a year in Japan, although it's unlikely that you'll even feel the majority of these. Start to worry when an earthquake measured on Japan's *shindo* scale starts to be less of a one and more like a five, six or seven. In Tokyo's Great Kanto Earthquake in 1923, over 100 000 people lost their lives; and some seventy-two years later, an earthquake killed more than 6 000 people in Kobe.

So why is Japan so prone to earthquakes? Well, the fact that it's got around one-tenth of the world's total number of volcanoes, along with its many **onsen** or hot springs, points to some pretty severe disturbances going on within its core. And indeed Japan is situated right above the point where several of the Earth's tectonic plates meet.

All of which explains why there are frequent televised reports detailing the evermore ingenious ways in which construction engineers are building earthquake-resistant homes and businesses.

It also provides a reason for why, on the anniversary of the Great Kanto Earthquake each year, Japan's **self-defence force** and paramedics practise an emergency drill in anticipation of Japan's long-overdue – given that earthquakes in Tokyo should technically occur about once every seventy years – 'big one'.

EATING

A bewildering array of *kata* is attached to the above activity, which is only partially understood/practised by many Japanese themselves. However, the following basic points may assist a *gaijin* to endear him/herself to their dining companion(s).

1. Before commencing dining, clasp your hands together as though in prayer, slightly bow your head and say '*Itadakimasu*'. (Ee-ta-da-ki-masu.) This has roughly the same meaning as 'For what I am about to receive, may I be grateful'.

2. It is likely that you will have a variety of shared dishes from which to choose. Don't pick up something with your *hashi* (chopsticks) and then change your mind and put it back. Deposit selected food on your own personal plate which

will have been given to you, along with your own rice bowl.

3. Don't pick up your plate, which contains selected food (i.e. *sashimi*), when eating from it. You can, however, do this with your rice bowl and (if served) soup.

4. Don't use your chopsticks to point at someone, or even something. A major *faux pas*. Also, don't leave chopsticks standing up in your rice bowl; Japanese Buddhists only do this when honouring their ancestors at household shrines.

5. Appreciation for your meal can best be signified by saying '*Oishii*' ('Tasty'). The Japanese are not, as a rule, noisy eaters.

6. When finished, say '*Gochisosamadeshita*' ('Go-chi-so-sama-deshi-ta'). It means something along the lines of 'I have eaten a feast'. A *gaijin*'s ability to say this correctly is genuinely admired by the Japanese. Don't say '*Gochisosamadeshita*' before everyone else has finished eating.

In conclusion – chopsticks and difficult lingo aside – the experience really isn't that daunting. Following the above few points, however, will ensure that you help create the necessary *wa* at the dining table.

Incidentally, it's not considered polite to eat whilst 'on the move' – i.e. walking along a street – or, generally speaking, on public transport.

EEYORE

Listen to the Japanese talking amongst themselves – especially those who are below the age of thirty – and you may well come to the conclusion that they possess some sort of bizarre fetish for the donkey from *Winnie-the-Pooh*. However, what can be pronounced exactly like the donkey's name is in fact *ii-yo*, or 'that's fine'. Just to let you know, as I am not the only *gaijin* who's initially been baffled upon overhearing this.

ELECTRIC TOILETS

Commonly encountered all over Japan. Pressing one button, should you so desire, warms your seat. Pressing another causes jets of water to gently cleanse those intimate nooks and crannies. If you're embarrassed about 'noises', the electric toilet upon which you are perched may emit the sound of running water, or birdsong, while you perform your business. A 'medical' toilet is apparently being developed, which will analyse a user's waste for any sign of diseases such as diabetes or bowel cancer. *Talking* toilets have even been mentioned, though quite what their topics of conversation will be is anyone's guess ('Hi there – how you doing today? Oh boy, do you seem desperate! That's it, get nice and comfy. Though you might want to check out the toilet-roll situation before you get started – the last person before you used quite a lot of paper. It's okay? Right then – chocks away, eh?').

It's not all fun and games, however. Recently, on three separate incidents, electric toilets made by the firm Toto burst into flames. Fortunately, none of these toilets were occupied at the time of their spontaneous combustion (caused by a faulty bidet function), although, declared a Toto spokeswoman helpfully, the '... fire would have been just under your buttocks'.

No s@*%, Sherlock!

ENGLISH, JAPANESE

Okay, the meaning of what's written in the window of my local *panya* (bakery) – *We sell you plenty tasted bread and cake for you enjoy! ' –* is basically obvious. Similarly, the sign by the entrance to the strangely named 'Bar Granddad' – *'Don't worry if come here alone. We serve you plenty cosy time and intoxication'.*

Sounds like my kinda place!

But then you encounter 'sentences' plastered across T-shirts worn by hip young men and women, consisting of words apparently thrown together at random. The following are just a few of the bizarre 'messages' I've hurriedly scribbled down, glimpsed on the fronts and backs of unsuspecting people in shopping centres and in the street, recorded here for posterity: *Cookie nuts crazy chick with empower jealousy, yeah!,* and *Sometime live just learned hard on the road too much,* and *Never saying back – world in space this time.*

And it's everywhere: on clothes, in shops, on food

packaging, posters – absolutely everywhere. English is cool in Japan, regardless of whether or not it makes any sense.

As a result, approximately every two minutes an English-speaking *gaijin* arrives at Narita airport, sees this corruption of their native language all around, and thinks something along the lines of, 'I can clean up here! All I have to do is offer my services to this shop or that manufacturer, to put their slogans into "good" English, and I'm bound to get paid a packet!'

Sadly, it never works out that way. Because Japanese English is Japanese English – it makes the product it's advertising seem 'cool' to the consumer, while also giving a reassurance that it is, at heart, Japanese. Perfect English would just make a product seem foreign, and therefore to be treated with caution. Sales would suffer; jobs would be on the line.

Besides which, there's American English, Australian English, Caribbean English – why not Japanese English? The fact that it often doesn't make any sense should be neither here nor there.

It's wonderful stuff: sheer poetry ... Almost.

ENKA

At some stage during your stay in Japan, you'll probably turn on a television to see a (typically) middle-aged man or woman clad in a *kimono*, fronting a full band which consists both of such 'modern' instruments as drums and electric guitars, as well as traditional Japanese instruments such as the *shamisen*. Whether male or female, whoever's singing will be wearing a plaintive expression, and you may well notice the almost excessively 'warbly' nature of their voice.

Well, that's *enka* – a traditional form of Japanese ballad singing. The subject matter of the lyrics is popularly claimed to reflect something along the lines of a 'sweet resignation towards life's misfortunes'. Though, if you ask me, it can all get a bit bloomin' depressing, packed full with references to death, the desertion of a lover, having a general lack of family and friends, being skint, etc.

Recently, however, a handsome young devil named 'Jero' has been pretty much turning the traditional *enka* 'scene' on its head. Jero (real name Jerome Charles White, Jr.) is an African-American from Pittsburgh, born in 1981, whose Japanese grandmother first began to teach him the lingo in which he would eventually sing. Following his graduation from the University of Pittsburgh, Jero came to Japan to teach English, but released his first single *Umiyuki* ('Ocean Snow') in February 2008.

Jero has a distinctly 'hip-hop' image, with baggy clothes and a cap worn at a jaunty angle. He also has a singing voice that has proved to be of huge appeal to many older Japanese (it also helps that Jero comes across as being a polite and intelligent individual). And his general image is credited with having caused something of an '*enka* renaissance' among younger generations, who had previously largely abandoned *enka* in favour of such other musical styles as rap and heavy metal. Now, if only he could make those lyrics a bit more cheerful ...

F

FUGU

Full name *takifugu* – the *kanji* characters for which read 'river pig' – a member of the pufferfish family. Although it carries the poison tetrodotoxin in its skin, its testicles and, particularly, its liver and ovaries (to say nothing about *fugu* also being extremely expensive) there are still many people who are rather fond of eating it.

For this reason *fugu* can only be prepared by specially trained chefs, using knives that are otherwise kept under lock and key. However, a certain number of people (estimates vary quite dramatically, from under ten victims per year to well over a hundred) do still fall ill and die after consuming *fugu*.

Most fatalities are believed to arise from an ill-advised desire to taste a little of the poison along with the flesh of the *fugu*, which is reputed to be quite bland. (I'm neither rich nor brave enough to try it myself.)

Ingesting just a little tetrodotoxin apparently livens up the proceedings by causing a 'prickling' sensation of the lips and tongue – which really does sound great, I have to say – though have too much and you can expect your circulatory and respiratory systems to shut down fairly rapidly.

In almost all cases where there is no medical intervention in the shape of a life-support machine – and even in some cases where there is – death by asphyxiation soon follows. However, some people have previously been known to recover from the total paralysis that mimics death – on a couple of occasions just before they were about to be cremated.

FUJI-SAN

Should really get a mention, given that it's probably Japan's most recognisable symbol after the *geisha*. The facts are, then, that Fuji-san lies almost exactly in the middle of Japan, and although classed as a volcano has been dormant since 1707 (which, if you're planning to climb it, will probably come as something of a relief).

Recognised since ancient times as a symbol of the divine, women were not permitted to climb Fuji until after the **Meiji Restoration**, which had something to do with the fact that only men were permitted to be priests and monks.

Nowadays, expect to see a fair amount of rubbish on your way up the mountain, with the surrounding forests in particular being well known as a 'fly-tipping' spot for unwanted furniture, freezers – even cars. And at the very top of Mount Fuji, alongside the 200-metre-deep crater, you'll find, to your undoubted delight, an assortment of neon-lit vending machines.

According to a well-known Japanese proverb, climbing Mount Fuji once makes you a wise man; climb it twice and you're a fool.

FURIN

You might see one of these hanging from the eave of a house – it's a small bell that's commonly constructed from glass or metal, and attached to its clapper is a strip of paper called a *tanzaku*. Upon this *tanzaku* there might be written a classical Japanese poem or verse – and when a light summer breeze catches the *tanzaku*, the bell emits a slight chime.

In spite of the delicacy of this chime, however, *furin* are not really to be found in built-up areas, as they don't half annoy the neighbours.

FUTON

A first-time visitor to Japan, transferring by coach from Tokyo's Narita airport to their hotel, or perhaps to the domestic airport Haneda for a connecting flight, can't help but be struck by the thousands of *futon* that have been placed out to air on the balconies of Tokyo's countless apartment blocks – assuming, of course, that it is a fine day.

Many 'beds' in Japan are made up of a *futon* covered by a sheet that is put out in the evening. Otherwise *futon* are kept in a cupboard known as *oshiire*, which serves to free up space in what are often slightly cramped living conditions.

You'll encounter *futon* rather than beds if you stay at a **ryokan** – a traditional Japanese inn – as opposed to a hotel.

G

GAIJIN

Shortened form of the word *gaikokujin*, which means 'outside country person'. A person born outside Japan will still be considered by most Japanese to be *gaijin* even after they have lived in the country for most of their lives, thus coming to understand the language and culture perfectly. Put it this way: you can have a seventy-year-old professor of ancient Japanese (or something of the sort), born in Oxford, England, but living in Japan since the start of the 1950s. He has a Japanese wife, and they have two grown-up children. The professor is, of course, completely fluent in Japanese; his wife jokes that he speaks it better than she.

When he dies the professor will have a Buddhist funeral, and his ashes will be interred in the family *haka*. He doesn't expect ever to go back to England again – it's a long flight, and anyway his family, friends, work and life in general are all in Japan.

Then one day – now in the autumn of his successful life, and while walking serenely to the university where he continues to lecture on a part-time basis – two schoolboys giggle and shout 'Herro!' and 'Zis iz a pen!' at him.

So go to Japan for anything longer than a holiday, and you will soon a) be driven mad, b) give up and go home, or c) resign yourself to the fact that you will be considered as an 'outside country person' for the remainder of your stay.

GAMBATTE

Beneath the polite, patient and often slightly reserved exterior of the 'typical' Japanese person there lurks a beast. This beast is at all times ready and alert for a challenge, although any outward indication will rarely be given.

This beast is the reason why Japanese students can get by on four hours' sleep when studying for exams and why the typical Japanese *sarariman* thinks nothing of staying at the office till ten o'clock at night, only to then apologise for his rudeness should he leave before his colleagues.

This beast can trace its roots right back to the dawn of the *samurai*, and their code of *bushidō*. It has at its heart the *samurai* 'do or die' philosophy: to commit to something – anything – wholly, and to succeed in this field or else to die in the attempt.

All of the above and much, much more – entire books have been written about the 'do or die' factor – is contained within one single word: *Gambatte*.

'*Gambatte*,' says the midwife to the mother about to give birth.

'*Gambatte*,' says the mother to the child as it takes its first faltering steps.

'*Gambatte*,' says the father to the teenager, as he studies beyond the point of exhaustion for the all-important university entrance examinations.

'*Gambatte*,' says the employer to the young man, now working for a firm that must pull out all the stops – and work all the hours – in order to secure an important contract.

And so it goes on, through generations, until the word is effectively etched on the heart of every new-born Japanese child before he or she even utters their first cry.

'*Gambatte*': 'do your best!' – and, by implication, never, ever give up, no matter how seemingly insurmountable the odds. Because to give up was a source of great shame to the **samurai**, and if you've read this far, you'll know how they dealt with that ...

GAME SHOWS, JAPANESE

Japanese game shows – of the physical rather than the mental variety – commonly involve four things: water (usually freezing), a number of contestants wearing silly costumes (who will invariably enter said water at some point), an audience of limited mental capability (who will act as though someone getting wet is the funniest thing they've ever seen) and a presenter (often male) who requires medication to control what is obviously a serious hyperactivity disorder.

It is interesting to note that Japanese game shows are never watched by small children, who find them tiresome in the extreme.

GAWPING

As a *gaijin* in Japan, whether you're black, white, Indian or whatever, expect a certain amount of the above. Understand that you're considered to be a bit of an oddity – something you begin to suspect when you land at Narita airport to see the signs for 'Japanese' and 'Aliens'. (The latter word is also written on my identity card, which is something all *gaijin* living in Japan have to carry round at all times on pain of death – or at least a severe warning down at the local police station.)

As an official 'Alien', therefore (Sting, eat your heart out), small children will often turn their heads through a 180-degree arc to follow your progress as you walk past them in the street. But they are kids, after all; far more disturbing are the adults who do the same thing. Make any attempt to communicate with these people –

by saying '*Konichiwa*' ('Hello'), or merely just by nodding and smiling – and they will do one of three things.

They will a) stagger back as though shot and then hurry away, all the while mumbling incoherently to themselves; b) give a reluctant grimace in response and then hurry away, all the while mumbling incoherently to themselves, or c) give an oddly relieved-sounding burst of laughter and perhaps even pat you on the arm, as though to confirm that you are, in fact, just another human being.

Thankfully, small children aside, gawpers are not encountered too often. Most Japanese are, after all, very polite people. But the longer you stay in Japan – and especially if you're living/holidaying in a more 'remote' and less cosmopolitan part of the country – the greater chance you have of feeling like E.T.

GEISHA

Originally, most *geisha* were male. Honest. From around 1200 they were the equivalent of Western jesters, amusing their *daimyō* (feudal lord) with storytelling, dancing and singing. Although they often had other, more serious, roles such as acting as advisors and confidants to their lord and master during times of conflict.

On occasion the *houkan*, as these male jesters were known, were even expected to march into battle at their masters' sides – to fight and if need be to die, just like your regular Joe soldier. Which is, if you ask me, rather unfair, as being able to tell the odd bawdy joke, coupled with the ability to spin a good yarn and maybe dance a bit, hardly prepares someone for the rigors of martial combat.

The first female *geisha* (only she was then called a *geiko*, or 'arts-girl') apparently caused quite a stir when she unveiled herself at a party around 1750, causing the *houkan* present to sulk and have a hissy fit. They realised that this ethereal creature, with her stunning red lips and lead-based white face paint, had just rung the death-knell for *houkan* everywhere.

Although a select few do still endure to this very day – if you know where to look for them ...

GENJI, THE TALE OF

The world's oldest book? Most academics would seem to think so. It was written by Murasaki Shikibu in the early tenth century, following the death of her husband and her transference to the court of the Empress Shoshi. Murasaki had apparently intended to become a nun but, to the great relief of tenth-century literature lovers everywhere, decided to write a novel instead.

Actually, before *The Tale of Genji* there was not a great deal of literature of which to speak. Well, there were certainly poems, a medium by which members of the 'upper classes' tended to communicate with one another – particularly their lovers. But an actual book, with things like a plot, character development and the like?

To be fair, the art of writing was greatly restricted by the limitations placed upon the Japanese by their sole use of the Chinese *kanji* system, which was only eased with the invention of *kana*.

Only women were supposed to use *kana* at first, and they certainly weren't expected to chance their arm at *kanji*, which remained the exclusive preserve of such learned men as priests.

Murasaki Shikibu, however, had a scholarly father who by all accounts was also a bit of a forward-thinking rebel. He therefore taught his daughter *kanji* along with her brother, something that would come in extremely useful in just a few years' time ...

Following the early death of her husband, Murasaki moved to the Empress's Court and began writing her epic tome (over 1 000 pages in the English translation). *The Tale of Genji* tells the story of a young man called – yep, you've got it – who is born into a royal court in Japan, where the Emperor quickly takes a shine to him.

Genji grows up proficient in the arts of etiquette, writing poetry, music, and other similar things considered to be of vital importance in ancient Japan. Renowned for his good looks, Genji soon has plenty of women chasing after him – but he is only interested in those who appear to be unobtainable. Much of the book concentrates on Genji's various affairs, and it is still today – both inside and outside of Japan – considered to be a fairly accurate representation of human desire, passion, jealousy and so forth.

Like Chaucer's *The Canterbury Tales* in England, *The Tale of Genji* is often featured in school textbooks and as part of the exam syllabus. Even for native Japanese speakers, however, it does require a fair bit of interpretation.

GESTURES

A hand held outstretched, palm face downwards with the fingers opening and closing, means 'Please come here'. The first finger, tip placed on its owner's nose, politely enquires: 'Are you talking/referring to me?' (It can also make that person resemble a toddler who's halfway through performing 'Simon Says'.) Two first fingers, pointing upwards and moved quickly back and forth by the owner's cheeks, is a humorous way for males to indicate that their significant other has recently been in a less than jovial mood. (I believe that this particular gesture is meant to represent an *oni*, or demon, though I've yet to receive any evidence in support of this. Certainly those Japanese I've asked don't have a clue one way or the other.)

After a while of experiencing the above, as well as an assortment of other weird and wonderful gestures, you may well come to the conclusion that they have been purposefully invented to baffle the average *gaijin*. And indeed you would, quite possibly, be correct.

GIRI

Of all the Japanese terms used to describe a certain type of behaviour, *giri* is perhaps the hardest to explain. Essentially *giri* means 'obligation' or 'duty', recognising the fact that it is impossible for a human being to live their life without falling into the debt of other people.

Indeed, the day we are born we already have debts: to our parents, firstly, and then to our family and finally to society in general. Therefore, we should not concern ourselves with trying to avoid something that is both as natural and inevitable as debt – be it financial, physical or mental – as someone in the West (which has a far more individualistic culture) might do.

Trying to follow *giri* and all of its social obligations can often place quite a strain on someone who is Japanese, especially when juxtaposed with their own wants and desires (seen as secondary in importance to the group as a whole).

To give a hypothetical example: when a person was desperate for employment in some particular field a few years previously, someone took a chance and took them on. Now that this person is fairly well known and established within his or her particular field (whatever it may be), they are being headhunted by another employer. This employer is offering both a promotion and a better salary, but still the person agonises over what to do. Should they accept the offer, deserting the person who originally gave them a chance and a job? Many would say yes, that it's just business, but such a course of action flies directly in the face of *giri* – which in this case requires the person to do his or her duty and remain with the employer who took them on in the first place.

Giri goes an awful lot deeper than this – entire books have been written on this subject alone – but the above example is one reason why Japanese workers have tended to remain with the same company their entire career, right up to retirement.

That's changing now, with a more Western approach to employment (i.e., it's okay to have a number of different employers within just a few years) being adopted by younger workers.

GLOVER, THOMAS

How did a nineteenth-century Scotsman, born in the tiny fishing village of Fraserburgh (later moving to Aberdeen), end up being awarded the 'Order of the Rising Sun' for all he'd done to benefit Japan?

Well, what's certain is that Glover was in Nagasaki by the time he was twenty-one, where he worked for a couple of years in the employ of Jardine, Matheson & Co., buying up Japanese tea for export as well as (rumour has it) dabbling in a bit of opium dealing on the side.

But Glover was too enterprising a soul to remain working for someone else for long, and so in 1861 he set up his own company called – with stunning originality – Glover & Co.

Speaking very generally, Glover & Co. were soon busy doing such things as shipbuilding, coalmining and introducing Japan to its first locomotive – the delicately named *Iron Duke*. Oh, and taking immediate sides in the uneasy state of affairs that was Japanese politics at the time, Glover also sold firearms to two rogue *samurai* clans who were opposed to the ruling Tokugawa Shogunate.

Shortly afterwards, the Westernised estate that Glover had built on a hillside overlooking Nagasaki Harbour became a refuge to some of those who were planning to bring about the **Meiji Restoration**.

The house where Glover and his family lived (entitled, just to avoid any confusion, Former Glover House) retains its two 'secret' rooms where, legend has it, the famous *samurai* swordsman **Ryōma Sakamoto** liked to conceal himself on occasion. (The Glover Gardens in Nagasaki, comprise several colonial-looking properties and surrounding grounds, and well worth a visit. They are open all year round.)

There remains a bust of the Italian composer Puccini within the Glover Gardens, as Glover's Japanese wife, Tsuru, was famously the inspiration behind *Madam Butterfly*. By all accounts, Glover idealised Tsuru, although this failed to prevent him from having an affair with a local *geisha*, the result of which was both a son and an attempted suicide on the *geisha*'s behalf when Glover broke things off. (The reputation that endures to this very day of Glover being an upright Victorian gentleman is – it has to be said – slightly tarnished by his frequent involvement in drugs, guns and concubines.)

Glover became bankrupt at one point, but with typical resilience soon bounced back. Due to his previously mentioned support of the **Meiji Restoration**, he was basically in Easy Street once the Emperor had been put back on his throne in the newly-named Tokyo.

Glover died in Tokyo (where he had another home) in 1911, although his name remains revered within Japan to this day. However, the son (also called Thomas) he had by the *geisha* met a tragic end.

Old, alone and unjustly accused by both the Japanese and the Americans of having been a spy during the Second World War (which had only just ended with the atomic bombing of Nagasaki), he took his own life on 26 August, 1945.

GOLF

In a country that's approximately 70 percent mountainous and has a population of well over 120 million – two factors that leave the average citizen feeling decidedly short of elbow room – why is a sport that requires so much land and space so popular?

Some say it appeals to the typical Japanese character; that it's so rigid in its *Zen*-inducing protocol and procedure that it's like some 'sporting' version of the **tea ceremony**. There is no heckling, no unseemly bodily contact, no need even to lose one's breath – golf can be played in a state of utter calm, a white-filtered Dunhill gripped between one's teeth if so desired.

Membership of a prestigious golf club has also – for years now – been viewed as something of a status symbol, along with the gas-guzzling American car and the Tokyo penthouse apartment. This is hardly surprising, as such is the demand for membership that annual fees can quite literally be the equivalent of several hundred thousand pounds.

For business reasons, it's not uncommon for a company to invest in such a membership. New and potential customers of some importance can therefore be wooed on the green, with a bite to eat and a few whiskies at the clubhouse to follow.

The average *sarariman*, therefore, is strongly encouraged to invest in a set of clubs, if he wishes to see advancement within his firm. It's deemed of absolutely no importance if he'd rather stick chopsticks in his eyes than play golf; this is business, and as the saying goes in Japan 'the customer is God'.

So if God wishes to talk turkey over a nine-iron, that's exactly what shall happen. And so once again,

the poor old *sarariman* is expected to oblige everybody
except himself.

H

HACHIKO

By Tokyo's Shibuya Station, there stands a life-sized bronze statue of a dog by which millions of Tokyoites have been arranging to meet since it was first put in place in 1934. So, what's the story behind the pooch? Well, from early 1924, an Akita dog by the name of Hachiko used to accompany his master – a professor at Tokyo University called Hidesamuro Ueno – to the train station in the morning, and would be there in the afternoon to greet Ueno's return from work. All was well until one day in May 1925, when the professor suddenly expired while giving a lecture. Unaware that his beloved master would no longer be returning home, Hachiko continued to wait at Shibuya Station for the following decade. (The station's employees were apparently quite fond of the mutt, giving it food, water and somewhere to sleep while presumably making sure that it didn't poop in the ticket hall.

Other accounts concerning Hachiko's life and times, however, claim that the dog appeared only in the afternoon, at exactly the time when the train Ueno would have caught home from work drew into the station.)

In March 1935, the faithful hound finally went to that great doggie heaven in the sky. (Hachiko's general fame had already caused the bronze statue of him to be put in place; Hachiko himself was purportedly there at its unveiling.) After Japan entered the Second World War, however, the statue was melted down so that its metal might be used for a more destructive purpose. But it was so sorely missed that – following the end of the war – a group calling itself The Society for Recreating the Hachiko Statue caused a second statue to be commissioned in 1948. Hachiko's stuffed and mounted remains, meanwhile, remain on display at Tokyo's National Science Museum. And at the time of writing, a film based upon the Hachiko story, starring Richard Gere as the dog's owner, is reportedly in production. (So, apologies if I just gave away the plot.)

HAIKU

In keeping with classic **Zen** simplicity, *haiku* is a form of poetry that's stripped bare of anything that might be considered superfluous. It obeys a strict five-seven-five syllable count, and is supposed to capture something plain and simple that can happen in a heartbeat – e.g. a frog jumping into a pond – while at the same time having profound philosophical implications that have the ability to stir something deep within the human soul. (Although I have yet to discover how this relates to the aforementioned frog and its pond.)

Or something like that, anyway – there seem to be almost as many different theories concerning how *haiku* should be interpreted as there are poems. However, common consensus does seem to bear out that one of the finest *haiku* poets of all time was a wandering monk called Basho – his pen name, apparently – who, during the latter part of the sixteenth century, spent a great deal of time sitting alone in a flea-infested hut (he can't have done that much 'wandering', then), while rattling off numerous *haiku*.

Which is great, I suppose, just so long as your main aim in life is to sit alone in a flea-infested hut and write *haiku*.

HANPO

Hanging within many a Chinese *Zen* temple (which are readily identifiable by their red-coloured *mon*, or main gate), you'll find a pair of large wooden drums that are shaped like fish. I've seen such a pair at the *Kofukuji Zen* temple in Nagasaki, which are – declares the guidebook written in English, presumably without a hint of bias – 'considered the most beautiful out of all the Zen temples in Japan ...'

Beautiful they may be, intact they're not. By which I mean that years of being struck in order to call the temple monks to work, and to tell them when it's time to eat, have left the bellies of the fish somewhat ... err ... disintegrated.

The larger, male fish has in its mouth a ball, which symbolises desire. This should be symbolically expelled each time the fish is struck. The female fish has a closed mouth, but, with its lips drawn back, still succeeds in displaying a fine array of sharp teeth.

You wouldn't let it nibble your fingers, put it that way.

HASHI

Chopsticks. Not the tune you play on the piano, but those implements used for eating in the Far East. *Hashi* can be highly deluxe and kept for life – some, for example, are made from ivory – but in most restaurants you'll be given a pair of 'half-split' chopsticks made from unfinished wood, which will be thrown away once you've finished your meal.

HATSUYUME

The first dream of the New Year (or, to be precise, from the night of New Year's Day to 2 January – because many people don't sleep at all from 31 December through to New Year's Day). It's deemed as being good luck to dream about (in no particular order) a) **Fuji-san,** b) hawks and/or c) aubergine.

Why? Well, Mount *Fuji* is Japan's highest mountain, a hawk is a strong bird, and aubergine were once (during the glory days of the *samurai*) extremely expensive – and thus symbolise impending wealth.

I mean, isn't it obvious?

HIBAKUSHA

I know two *hibakusha* myself – namely, my wife's grandmother (seventy-seven at the time of writing) and my *judō* instructor (seventy-nine or eighty, depending on when you ask him).

My wife's grandmother was working in an underground factory in Nagasaki when the Americans dropped 'Fat Man' at 11.02 a.m. on 9 August, 1945. Nakamura-*sensei* (the *judō* instructor) was a soldier stationed in the city, and saw the explosion with his own eyes. 'A big ... bang,' he described to me once in halting English. 'A big ... light.'

That my wife's grandmother was underground and Nakamura-*sensei* the necessary distance away from the explosion's hypocentre (approximately 70 000 people weren't – and they're the ones who died instantly) are facts that saved both their lives.

Still, that they were in the vicinity of the explosion

on that fateful day has ever since caused them to be classified as *hibakusha* – literally 'explosion-affected people'. This entitles them to a certain amount of money each month from the government, and whatever medical treatment they require entirely free of charge (my wife's grandmother, to give an example, contracted anaemia within a few weeks of the explosion – something that she declares was a relatively mild side-affect).

However, for years following the war, *hibakusha* and their children (who were also classified *hibakusha*) experienced prejudice and discrimination, sometimes treated as though they had a disease communicable by touch, and on occasion being refused employment in case they should suddenly sicken with radiation poisoning – even many years after the bombings of Nagasaki and Hiroshima.

HIGAN

If you're a Japanese Buddhist, you believe that when a person dies their spirit heads west, beyond where the sun sets. This fact is celebrated twice a year, for a period of seven days each time. *Haruhigan* takes place in March (*haru* meaning spring), while *akihigan* occurs during October (*aki* being autumn).

During the seven-day period of both *higan*, the time taken from when the sun rises in the east to when it sets in the west is exactly twelve hours. Therefore, darkness and light briefly exist in two perfectly equal halves.

At sunset over this special period, Japanese Buddhists – *Higan* is particular to Japanese Buddhism – pray towards the west, thereby honouring the souls of their ancestors. They – the people praying that is, not the ancestors – also go to the family *haka* (a Buddhist tomb) to serve flowers and *okashi*, which can basically be whatever the deceased person or persons being honoured liked to eat or drink in their lifetime. And, yes – on more than one occasion I've seen placed beside a *haka* a packet of crisps and a couple of cans of beer.

HINOMARU

The national flag of Japan. *Hinomaru* means 'sun circle', which basically describes the large red dot that's in the centre of an otherwise white flag. (This dot, incidentally, must be *exactly* in the centre of the flag, its diameter three-fifths of the flag's height.)

Hinomaru purportedly dates back as far as the twelfth century, when various *samurai* clans were fond of displaying it on banners and fans.

Hinomaru, incidentally, is also the name given to the *obento*, or boxed lunch, that consists of nothing more fancy than white rice with a red pickled plum (an *umeboshi*) in the centre. Fancy-free but very nutritious (so

long as you can stomach the pickled plum), it was the staple diet for Japan's poor during times of famine and economic hardship.

HOSUTESU BAR

Let's just imagine that you're in the centre of Tokyo for one evening only, with a great big wad of yen that you absolutely, positively must use up before dawn. What would you do? How would you spend it?

Well, if you're male and enjoy the company of beautiful, immaculately groomed women who will treat everything you say as though it's either the wittiest or the most profound thing they've ever heard, whilst at the same time making sure that your glass is never empty (and lighting your cigarette if you smoke), then you could try visiting what is known as a *Hosutesu* Bar.

I mentioned Tokyo at the start of this entry, but hostess bars can be found all over Japan, and particularly in the 'entertainment district' of every major city. They usually cost a small fortune to enter (which helps keep out the riffraff), and once inside you'll continue to pay through the nose for alcohol and female company.

It's common to find women of all nationalities working in hostess bars, even if they speak next to no Japanese. Blonde, blue-eyed women are particularly in favour, but all that's really required from the 'hostess' is that she looks good, listens attentively to everything her customer tells her – although she may not understand any of it – and encourages as much money to be spent as is humanly possible.

Incidentally, male versions of *Hosutesu* bars have, of late, come into fashion, where immaculately groomed young men cater to women who are in possession of a large disposable income.

1

IGO

This board game has the usual three-step history common to so many things to do with Japan: it first came from China (in this case around the eighth century), and was then played purely by the nobility until the hoi polloi at last managed to get their mitts on it.

The grid-like *igo* board has exactly 361 intersecting points, and is played using a couple of stones that are coloured either white or black. The least skilled player uses the black stones, and is allowed to start the game.

If a player manages to surround their opponent's stone with enough of their own, then that stone becomes forfeit. And the person who takes the most stones, strangely enough, wins the game.

IKEBANA

The 'arrangement of flowers', *ikebana* or *kadō* (literally 'the way of flowers') is an art form that can trace its roots – sorry – all the way back to the sixth century, when priests in Buddhist temples offered flowers to honour Buddha as well as the spirits of the dead.

By the sixteenth century, however, everyone was practising *ikebana*. Even the macho **samurai** could often be found trying his hand at the standard *rikka* style, or debating (perhaps with his feudal lord) the merits of the relatively new *nageire* way of arranging that had evolved along with the **tea ceremony**.

Like so much to do with Japan, *ikebana* looks deceptively simple. Its finest practitioners, however, may have spent up to five years in *ikebana* classes, learning all about colour combinations, the best use of natural shapes and lines, the ancient representations (through the arrangement of flowers) of heaven, earth and humankind, and much, much more.

Of course, that just completes their *training*. They'll require the rest of their lives to develop their art.

INARI

In any part of Japan, you're all but certain to come across an *Inari* shrine. You'll recognise it instantly by the pair of stone fox statues that are stood guard either side of the entrance or main *torii* – the particularly 'oriental'- looking couple of pillars (commonly painted red or orange at an *Inari* shrine) that are joined at the top by two cross pieces.

So, who exactly is *Inari*, and what's with the stone foxes?

The first thing you need to know is that *Inari* is the *kami* (or god) of rice. Therefore, keeping *Inari* happy is pretty darned important to the Japanese, given that rice is an absolute staple of most meals. In times gone by, a successful rice harvest made the difference between survival and starvation. It had the same importance to the Japanese as a good potato crop had to the Irish.

But what about *Inari* him-, her- or (and I mean this with the utmost respect) itself? Can we put a face to the name? Well, in this case it just so happens that we can, although when it comes to many **Shinto kami**, you won't always be so fortunate.

Inari is commonly depicted in one of two ways: either 'he' is an elderly man, usually bearded and carrying a couple of bundles of rice, or else 'she' is – and here I quote my Buddhist head-priest brother-in-law – 'a beautiful fox-faced young woman'.

Next question: what's with the foxes? Well, foxes are good for the rice harvest, y'see – they eat other animals that would otherwise damage it, like field mice and birds. In fact, a long, long time ago, a group of foxes went to see *Inari* to pledge themselves as his servants. I can only imagine that working for a *kami* was a hell of a lot more exciting than scratching around in dustbins at one in the morning.

'Keep an eye on the rice crop,' *Inari* told them, so that's just what they've been doing ever since.

Every year, the *Inari* shrine that's close to my home in Nagasaki has its own mini 'festival' in honour of the *kami* and his/her/its harvest-protecting foxes. A mass of people crowd the stairs leading up to the shrine, to watch as two men dressed in white fox outfits scale two ten-metre-high bamboo poles. Hence the reason this occasion is called *takengea* – literally, 'bamboo skill'.

At the very top of these poles the men rock backwards and forwards, several monks supporting the bottom of the pole in case it should suddenly 'pop' out of its supporting bracket. (Clearly, the health and safety element of this occasion has not evolved greatly in the many centuries since it began.)

The highlight for the audience comes when the fox-dressed acrobats throw out towels and sweets, which have until now been concealed within their white tunics. There then comes an even greater surprise (for those who are watching this for the first time, anyway) – a live chicken is produced and thrown down to the ground, to be caught by some lucky person and taken home to be plucked, cooked and eaten.

IRASHAIMASE

Probably the first word you will hear when you go shopping in Japan. Anyone working in a supermarket, department store, fast-food restaurant, even a post office or bank – in fact, most places that deal with Joe Public – is required to say '*irashaimase*' ('Welcome') about, oh, 70 000 times per day.

Staff in such places need to greet every new customer
– potential or otherwise – with '*irashaimase*', and in a
tone of voice that really does sound as though seeing
you has just *totally* made their day. And you know
what? I've never once heard a tired-sounding
irashaimase, or even one that's slightly half-hearted,
just a wee bit 'it's five o'clock on a Friday afternoon
and I really have had enough of work this week'. This
in itself, speaks volumes about the Japanese character.

The *ichiba* (market) stall-holders, in particular, have
a way of bellowing '*A-irashai-a-irashai-odozo*' at you
that makes you feel as though you've just made a salt-
of-the-earth drinking buddy; someone who would
gladly shout you a few cups of *sake* and some grilled
squid at a local *akachochin* or 'red-lantern' bar.

I could be mistaken in this impression, however.

ISHIHARA, SHINTARO

Governor of Tokyo since 1999, *Ishihara* is infamous
for his right-wing views and his frequent habit of putting his foot firmly in his mouth. Detested by television
personality and *gaijin* Dave Spector (*See* Spector,
Dave) for his racist and sexist comments, *Ishihara* has
previously declared that, instead of allowing Africans
into Japan, '... we should be letting in people who are
intelligent', and has suggested that women shouldn't be
allowed to live '... after they have lost their reproduc-
tive purposes'.

Ishihara also remarked that Japan should conduct 'pre-emptive' missile strikes on North Korea and China, and stated that the 1937 Rape of Nanking had been 'made up' by the Chinese. In the summer of 2005, he was sued by a number of French teachers living in Tokyo, after he decreed that their language '... can't count numbers'. *Ishihara's* considered opinion was based upon the fact that, in French, ninety is counted as *quatre-vingt-dix*, or 'four-twenty-ten'. (In Japanese it is *ku-ju* – 'nine-ten'.)

Ishihara ultimately won the case, with the judge declaring that although the governor's comments had 'lacked consideration', this didn't automatically mean that he'd damaged the French 'sense of honour'. Said a customarily defiant *Ishihara* afterwards: 'People can't sue me just because they don't like what I say'.

They can call him *baka* (an idiot or fool), however, and indeed quite frequently do.

J

JANKENPON

Whose turn is it to wash the dishes, go to the shops, or get up to let the cat out? Well, you can always settle such disputes with a quick game of *jankenpon* – 'scissors, paper, stone', basically.

Make a fist with your hand, and pull it back towards your body at the same moment as saying '*Janken*'. Then reveal your choice of scissor, paper or stone at exactly the same moment as you say, '*Pon.*'

Simple, really.

JAYWALKING

Nothing, to my mind, sums up the almost universal respect the Japanese have for law and order, than the sight of a great crowd of people waiting to cross a completely empty road. Even at two o'clock in the morning, they simply *will not* go until they see that green man (who, in my neck of the woods – Nagasaki – wears a hat, and sports a fine pair of flared trousers). Jaywalkers are almost always either impatient *gaijin* or less mature (i.e. younger) members of the *yakuza*, who seem to think that swaggering across a road while the red man is still showing will cause everyone watching to gasp at their sheer bravado.

Though I have to admit that – at least in the early hours of the morning – I have, on a couple of occasions, been that impatient *gaijin*.

JINJA

A *Shinto* shrine. These were originally somewhat simple affairs: a *kami* (or god) was recognised through the presence of something like an unusually large tree, or a strangely shaped rock, which was thus enshrined by wrapping a sacred straw rope round it. Only later were actual 'buildings' constructed beside the object or place considered holy, probably after the introduction of Buddhism and its temples to Japan.

JOZU

If you're a *gaijin* living in Japan, you're going to be hearing this word a lot. Learn more than two words of Japanese (*hai* – 'yes' – and *konichiwa* – 'good afternoon' – for example) and your Japanese friend/business associate/language student/whatever will praise your linguistic abilities as being '*Jozu ne!*' Ditto if you manage to use chopsticks even semi-correctly.

However, what approximately translates as 'skilful' is at times (you soon begin to realise) used ironically, and not always with the utmost sincerity. Thus an old-hand *gaijin* living in Japan soon develops a slight facial tick upon hearing that damn word, and learns to dismiss it with a curt '*Iie*' ('No').

It's painful to say, but you realise that you've become at least partly accepted by the Japanese when you stop being 'praised' with *jozu*.

JUDŌ

Once upon a time, if a *samurai* suddenly found himself on the battlefield denuded of both his horse and a weapon, he would rely on the ancient martial art of *jujutsu* in a bid to stay alive. *Jujutsu* boasted throws that were designed to – at the very least – permanently cripple an opponent, along with pressure-point blows delivered with the hands and feet. If applied with accuracy, such blows fully justified their title of being 'one strike, certain death'.

By the time of the **Meiji Restoration**, however, *jujutsu* had quite fallen from favour. Rather than being the *samurai*'s secret system of unarmed combat, it was now commonly employed by thugs, thieves and all manner of other ne'er-do-wells to terrorise the weaker (and also law-abiding) members of society.

One *jujutsu* practitioner, however, born in 1860, was an earnest and not-at-all-thuggish young student named Jigoro Kano. Although dismayed by *jujutsu*'s poor reputation and bewildered by its many 'forms', Kano trained so hard that he was, by his early twenties, a genuine expert. Indeed, it's commonly reported how he'd unconsciously wrestle with his bedcovers while asleep, so obsessed was he with practising.

Finally, Kano set about creating a 'new' martial art that would again appeal to Japan's populace – a phoenix arising from *jujutsu*'s ashes, as it were. It would be hard and lifelike, only lacking (or changing) the many moves that made *jujutsu* a martial art in which it was dangerous to train at even a basic level. (For example, *ippon-seoi-nage* – *judō*'s 'one-armed shoulder throw' that is today safely taught to every beginner – is derived from a *jujutsu* move that shattered an opponent's elbow.)

Soon *judō*'s popularity was widespread, not only within Japan but in other countries as well, while the Kodokan – the '*judō* headquarters' established by Kano in Tokyo – continues to exist to this day.

However, Kano – a peaceable man at heart, and one deeply opposed to the rabid right-wing militarism that grew within Japan during the 1930s – was strongly opposed to the government's demand that he train soldiers in his martial art. He'd no desire to help to create hardened thugs for a country that seemed ever more likely to side with Nazi Germany. So when Kano died (aged seventy-eight), purportedly from pneumonia, while on board a ship returning from Egypt in 1938, there was deep suspicion that he had in fact been assassinated by government agents tired of his continual, outspoken opposition of a Japan that was moving rapidly towards the Second World War.

JUKEN JIGOKU

Exam hell! 'Pass on four hours' sleep, fail on five' students are informed as they swat desperately for the forthcoming university entrance examinations.

As an interesting (and also slightly bizarre) footnote, that English item of confectionary the 'KitKat' has become popular with revising students – apparently due to the sound of its name, which is uncannily similar to *kitto katsu*, which can be interpreted as something like 'I hope you will succeed'. In honour of this, a couple of years ago Nestlé Japan brought out a special flavour of KitKat exclusively for their home market: green tea flavour. Yum!

JUZU

A bit like the Catholic rosary, *juzu* ('counting beads', also called *nenju*) are held while praying to Buddha. As the warrior monk Rennyo put it sometime during the fourteenty century: 'Praying without nenju lacks respect and is like grabbing the Buddha with your bare hands.'

Juzu commonly have 108 beads – a number that represents the amount of *bonnō*, or earthly desires, that a dedicated Buddhist must seek to overcome – and may also be worn as a protective charm against evil spirits. Old or broken *juzu* may be disposed of only by a **Shinto** priest, as part of a special ceremony.

К
_____

KABUKI

Traditional Japanese theatre, which first achieved popularity through the difficulties some merchants were having with the *samurai*. These merchants in Edo-era Japan – which lasted from the beginning of the sixteenth century right up until the **Meiji Restoration** – were becoming a little too wealthy, which really didn't please the *samurai,* who as warriors were supposed to be of a higher class than the merchants, but who were often so poor that they had to make do without eating.

As the poor old merchants couldn't really say 'Get stuffed!' or something of the sort when they got pushed around by the *samurai* – at least, not if they wished to keep their heads attached to their necks – they sought solace in *kabuki* plays that commonly depicted the struggle of ordinary people against the mean old feudalistic system.

Kabuki plays were, in those days, somewhat bawdy

events, with the female actors (who often doubled as prostitutes) accustomed to receiving the odd ribald remark or two from the audience 'pits'.

Finally the authorities did what they always do whenever it looks as though the proles are having too much fun: they sought to end the source of their amusement, this time by banning women from the *kabuki* stage, their roles from now on to be performed by men. Soon enough this became an integral part of *kabuki* (like a young woman playing the part of Aladdin in the traditional British pantomime), and so it's remained.

Oh, hang on ... Who are those *ninja*-like figures in the background of the stage, moving silently around? Oh, *them*. They shift scenery, prompt the odd line – things like that. You're supposed to ignore them, and after a few minutes that's exactly what you find your-self doing.

KAMIKAZE

A word commonly associated with the suicidal Japan-ese fighter pilots of the Second World War, who delib-erately smashed their planes into Allied shipping vessels. And indeed *kamikaze* ('divine wind') has become synonymous with any type of suicidal attack from the air, most notably the 11 September attacks.

But long before any of this, in the dim and distant

days of 1274, the feared Mongol chieftain Kublai Khan
sent a force to invade Japan. The Mongols easily captured some outlying Japanese islands before landing at
Hakata Bay, and, despite the savage bravery of the
Japanese *samurai*, soon began to make significant
progress inland.

And then something strange happened – that same
evening the invading force returned to their waiting
ships. It's been suggested that they intended to renew
their attack the following day; but that night a fierce
storm blew up which scattered the fleet and left thousands of men drowned.

The Japanese gave heartfelt thanks to the *kamikaze*,
which would save their bacon once more seven years
later. Again it was those pesky Mongols who were
attempting to invade (Kublai Khan was noted for his
persistency), and again they easily captured some outlying islands before landing at Hakata Bay.

This time, however, the Japanese *samurai* managed
to hold off the invading force for almost two months,
though their hearts quailed as rumours reached
them that some 100 000 men, being transported by
over 3 000 ships, were on their way from China.

But just around this time – as the invading force
based out at sea really *was* starting to enlarge, rumour
or no rumour – another typhoon sprang up.

'Bloody Japanese weather!' snarled the surviving
Mongolian, Chinese and Korean soldiers and sail-

ors, as they set their battered boats on a course for home.

KANA

In order that they might commit their words to paper (or scroll), the Japanese originally relied on imported Chinese *kanji*. *Kanji* was, however, often ill suited to the polysyllabic language of the Japanese, particularly when expressing grammatical tenses – a fact that frequently caused confusion among the few people (for example priests) who were literate.

Around the ninth century, however, *kana* came along and solved all these niggling little problems. Some say that this phonetic script was developed by a monk called Kūkai, although it was slow to be taken up by anyone except for women (especially Murasaki Shikibu and her *Tale of Genji* (See **Genji, The Tale of**), who from the early tenth century used *kana* to write a series of lively novels based around sex and everyday power-struggles – a sort of *Desperate Housewives* or *Sex and the City* for the age.

'Huh!' sneered the learned monks. 'Just *look* at the sort of trash *kana*'s being used to write. Think we'll just stick with good old *kanji*, thank you very much!'

Kana consisted of two different types – *hiragana*, for native Japanese words and grammatical structures; *katakana*, for imported words like 'David Beckham'

(*See* **Beckham, David**), or whomever it was that was causing Japanese teenagers to wet their knickers in the ninth century.

However, over the next couple of hundred years, *kanji* and *kana* came naturally together to form the wonderful language that is Japanese – which, at any given moment, has millions of *gaijin* laughing hysterically at the very idea that they might one day be able to master it.

KANJI

Some are relatively simple. 山 or *yama*, for example, does actually quite look like a mountain. Ditto 雨 or *ame* (rain). But then you also have something like 薔薇 , which to my mind doesn't look anything *like* a *bara* (rose).

Kanji was originally pinched from China around the sixth century, when the Japanese language had no written form of its own. There are estimated to be about 80 000 *kanji* in total, although most of these are so obscure that they are used in neither the Japanese nor the Chinese writing systems.

In Japan you need to come to know and love about 2 000 of these little devils – along with their various meanings, depending on how they're being used – to be able to read and understand your average daily 新聞 or *shimbun* (newspaper).

It's a damn sight harder than learning the ABC, anyway.

KAPPA

If there was an annual award for the 'Country with the Strangest-Looking Mythological Creatures', I have little doubt that Japan would win hands down. They've got the *tengu* (of which there are two types), the *oni* and also the *kappa*.

But how do you describe a *kappa*? Well, the simplest way I think (and just bear with me here) is to imagine Mr Burns from *The Simpsons* with a ring of spiky hair around a water-filled crater on top of his head. Add a beak, green instead of yellow skin, a tortoise-like shell on his back and some seriously webbed fingers and toes, and you've pretty much got your average, common-or-garden *kappa*.

Kappa are hungry little blighters who delight in eating the entrails of cattle and horses, which they suck out through the animal's ... Actually, maybe that's more information than you need (or should I say *want*) to know.

What a *kappa* finds *really* tasty, however, is a human being. And while only being the size of the average six- to seven-year-old child, *kappa* are incredibly strong due to the water they keep in the crater that's on top of their heads. (It's all to do with magic, see')

Thus, even a full-grown man, venturing past a remote lake or stream (*kappa* tend to hang out where there's water in abundance), may be challenged to *sumo*-style combat by an odd-looking creature with a strong smell of fish about his person. Faced with such danger, what would you do? Well, if you've a cucumber in your possession (unlikely, granted, but then you never know) you can offer it to the *kappa*, as cucumber is his number-one favourite food. And while he's scoffing said vegetable, you can beat a hasty retreat.

Even if you *don't* have a cucumber, however, never fear. When not sucking the entrails out of animals and humans in quite a ... unique ... way, *kappa* are actually quite polite creatures. In other words, bow to them and they'll feel obliged to bow right back.

This, of course, causes the magic, strength-giving water that's in the saucer on top of their heads to spill out, meaning that they're suddenly left feeling rather weak, and will beg you not to harm them.

If you can restrain the urge to say 'Hang on a moment – a minute ago you were all set to suck out my entrails, and now you're trying to appeal to my compassionate side? Not a chance, pal – you're for it!' then you can make the *kappa* promise anything, as breaking a promise is something the *kappa* can never do.

Having a *kappa* at one's mercy is exactly the sort of

situation in which a 'raincoat dealer' (whatever the hell that is) called Ichiro once found himself.

'If I ever need any assistance,' Ichiro told the creature grovelling in front of him, 'you'd better help me out.'

'Yes, yes – anything you say, master,' replied the *kappa*.

'Okay – we'll leave it at, then,' said Ichiro.

A few years passed, until one day Ichiro decided to build a vast drainage system close to the lake where he'd once encountered the *kappa*. Exactly *why* a raincoat dealer should suddenly decide to construct a vast drainage system by the side of a remote lake has never been made entirely clear, but then I suppose stranger things have happened ...

Anyway, let down by friends and family members who'd said that they'd help him, only to then suddenly remember prior commitments, Ichiro was slowly drained of all his physical strength and financial fortune. At his lowest ebb, bent double over a pickaxe, Ichiro at last remembered the promise he'd extracted from the *kappa*. He also realised that he was working within just a few metres of the water's edge – did the *kappa* still inhabit the lake ...

'Kappa, if you still be there, come and make good on your promise,' called Ichiro in suitably solemn tones.

Almost at once the *kappa* appeared, looking shifty and trying to pretend that he'd not noticed all this work that was taking place right beside his patch.

'I'd have helped you out from the start, if only I'd known ...' declared the *kappa*, without much conviction.

This story ends rather abruptly – as you're about to find out – with the *kappa* filling the crater on top of his head with water, and so with superhuman strength finishing the entire job by himself.

KAPUSERU HOTERU

'Capsule hotel' that offers coffin-like chambers, commonly stacked two high, in which to sleep. If you can sleep, that is – what with the near-continual coming and going of customers, *kapuseru hoteru* tend to be a bit noisy.

The curtain at the entrance to your plastic or fibreglass sleeping chamber can be drawn for privacy, while personal possessions are stored within a locker.

Kapusera hoteru have at least the advantage of being reasonably cheap, although foreign backpackers who are low on funds, and are hoping to get a good night's sleep in one, are often turned away by xenophobic managers who've previously had to deal with one belligerent and non-Japanese speaking *gaijin* too many.

A common resident of a *kapusera hoteru* is the *sarariman* who's once again missed the last train home due to an enforced late-night drinking session with the boss.

KARAOKE

Can be translated (rather peculiarly, I think) as 'empty orchestra'. *Karaoke* can commonly be found in **Hostesu bars**, though just as widespread – and about a million *yen* cheaper – are the *karaoke* rooms where groups of friends sit gathered around a large screen, punching their selection into the controller and taking turns to sing.

Depending on the amount paid when booking the room for a two- or three-hour stretch, by the way, unlimited drinks and snacks are often provided courtesy of the management.

This never fails to put a smile on my face, anyway.

KARŌSHI

Literally 'death from overwork' – the sort of thing that tends to occur when companies expect their employees to work sixteen hours a day, seven days a week.

An exaggeration? Japan's spectacular recovery from the destruction visited upon it by the Second World War, to become a major economic power within barely thirty years, did not come about without its workforce performing some *serious* (and largely unpaid) overtime.

This is one of the main criticisms of Japan's **gambatte** culture – the constant, competitive desire many Japanese people have to outperform their colleagues at work, or even their own performance the previous week or day. *Gambatte,* therefore, makes them amenable to major exploitation at the hands of their employers – or this is how it would seem to many in the West.

For some years now, however, younger Japanese workers have been becoming more vocal in demanding a better life/work balance. Largely gone are the days when apparently healthy men in their twenties and thirties were dropping dead of heart attacks and strokes, caused by the unrelenting stress and crushingly long hours of their job.

But many of the 'old guard' of Japan's economic workforce continue to work long hours, seeing themselves as the last line of defence against what they perceive to be the increasingly lazy, slovenly (and in this case often Western) ways of the younger workers.

In any case, differences between young and old aside, anyone coming to Japan will quickly realise that its workforce remains one of the most diligent, as well as efficient, in the world.

KATA

Japan is a country built upon *kata* – a ritualised way of doing something that is deemed to be the most efficient. Most Western people know of *kata* through the martial arts, with *karate*, for example, having various styles of pre-determined movements that must be learned in order to attain a higher grade.

Kata is slightly on the wane now – especially among younger people – but in the days of the *samurai* there was *kata* for almost everything – eating, drinking, work, meeting people, writing (for example, the order of the intricate strokes needed to create *kanji* characters – this was, of course, in the days when they didn't have word processors) and a great deal else.

KATORISENKO

Japan's exceptionally hot and humid summers bring out a common enemy of mankind. Namely, the dreaded mosquito. Smear your skin with as many brands of repellent as you like; they will all have only a limited effect against you being eaten alive.

If you truly wish to avoid having to scratch yourself like a leper on speed, then you have only one real choice: get yourself a *katorisenko*. That's a green coil, about six inches wide, which you set alight before placing in a round, shallow tin with a perforated lid. The *katorisenko* slowly burns, emitting copious quantities of incense-like smoke. You will see nearly all gardeners wearing two such tins strapped to their belt on either side of their waist. And they work, they really do.

KAWARA

Roof tiles – commonly grey, but on occasion green, blue or brown – that were in use as long ago as the seventh or eighth century. They come in a variety of shapes and sizes – in particular, look out for the gargoyle-like *oni* tiles that adorn the corners of some temples and other, old-style Japanese buildings, which reputedly serve to drive away evil spirits.

KAWASHIMA, RYUTA

Born on May 23, 1959, Professor Kawashima is an internationally renowned neuroscientist whose work can best be described (to dullards such as myself) as being broadly concerned with 'mapping the human brain'. His *Train Your Brain: 60 Days to a Better Brain* was first published in Japan in 2003, and featured a collection of such mental exercises as quizzes. Printed in English in 2007, *Train Your Brain* has gone on to sell well over two million copies. It has also been adapted for the Nintendo DS portable console, with celebrities such as Nicole Kidman being used to advertise the assorted benefits of giving the ol' grey matter a workout.

Professor Kawashima seems to be a genuinely altruistic individual. Although he could have become an extremely wealthy man from his 'sideline' of books and computer games, he declares that he has taken 'not one yen' in royalties. All the money generated is instead ploughed back into the university where he conducts his research, buying better equipment, paying for more staff, and so on.

KEIGO

Honorific language – or, to translate it exactly, 'respectful language'. *Keigo* gives rise to a bewildering amount of verb and sentence endings, which are fully understood by only a few Japanese people themselves. It comes from the days when you spoke differently to a *samurai* than you did to the local fish-stall holder, for so long as you quite valued your insides remaining that way.

Very basically, part of *keigo* entails the speaker referring to him- or herself in suitably humble terms, while treating the person they are talking to with god-like reverence. This is especially true in business, or when meeting someone perceived to be of a higher social status for the first time.

Use *keigo* incorrectly, and it's possible to mortally offend someone by offering a cup of *cha* instead of *ocha* (the 'o' here being honorific). However, don't worry about it if you're a *gaijin*, as it's yet another thing you're not supposed to know the slightest thing about.

KEMPEITAI

Founded in early January 1881, Japan's 'military police' were intended mainly to enforce recent conscription legislation introduced by the Meiji government. This had proved particularly unpopular amongst peasant families, who could hardly afford for healthy young sons to be taken away from the land.

It was during the 1930s, however, that the *Kempeitai* really began their reign of terror. (Although during the annexation of Korea by Japan in 1910, the *Kempeitai* had been notorious for their violent repression of any anti-Japanese sentiment.) In a three-year period alone, they had arrested over 60 000 people for having 'dangerous thoughts'. During the Second World War, they helped supervise prisoner-of-war camps, actively participating in innumerable atrocities. In the 'Asian Auschwitz' of Pingfan, China, Unit 731 – a biological and chemical warfare development operation formed by the *Kempeitai* – murdered over a quarter of a million Chinese in hideous experiments.

The *Kempeitai* was disbanded in 1945, following the American occupation of Japan.

KENDAMA

A more developed version of the 'cup and ball' so beloved of children in Victorian times, *kendama* has a handle with two shallow 'cups' on either side (along with a smaller one at the base) and a prong at the top that fits inside a small hole bored inside the ball.

Getting the prong to enter the ball is, of course, one of the most advanced tricks of the *kendama* – ensure that the ball is absolutely still, and then flick it up while at the same time positioning the 'prong' directly underneath it. After about 20 000 failed attempts, you should be able to perform the trick flawlessly.

KI

Okay, I'm going to sound a bit 'hippy-dippy' here for a moment. Just bear with me, will you?

Ki is the life force – an indefinable source of energy – that exists in everything living. By 'living' also include here the supernatural, as for example '天気 or *tenki*, the Japanese for weather – literally 'heaven's spirit'.

Martial artists commonly ascribe their feats of breaking or **tameshiwari** to *ki*, which is developed and honed through intensive breathing and posture exercises.

Despite some claims to the contrary, however, *ki* fireballs that are shot out through the hands of some wizened-looking martial arts master really don't occur in real life.

Just wanted to make that *perfectly* clear.

KIMONO

Believed to have originated within Japan sometime around the tenth century, *kimono* ('something worn') usually consisted of numerous layers and were thus often extremely hot, heavy and generally bothersome to wear.

The nineteenth-century *kimono* had fewer layers, but it still experienced a drop in popularity when, due to the **Meiji Restoration**, Western clothing came somewhat into vogue.

Today, many women can be seen wearing a *kimono* as they go about their daily business, with the pattern of the *kimono* often reflecting the season – a floral pattern, for example, being popular during the spring.

Male *kimono* tend to be of a dark colour – grey or brown – and on special occasions a *kimono* bearing the family crest may be worn.

With both male and female *kimono*, a special type of white sock (a *tabi*) is worn. This has a separate 'socket' for the big toe, allowing the type of Japanese sandal that is called *zori* to be worn.

KNIFE, SHONEN

With founding members and sisters, Naoko and Atsuko Yamano, *Shonen Knife's* much-praised 2006 album *Genki Shock!* featured typically bizarre lyrics. One song, for example, praises the taste of broccoli, while another extols the virtues of the humble rubber band. (Daft song titles also abound, with such gems as *Banana Chips*, *Buttercup [I'm a Supergirl]* and the utterly brilliant – in all sincerity, it's one of my favourite songs – *Twist Barbie*, with its English-language refrain '... I wanna be twist Barbie ...' *Shonen Knife* frequently switch between Japanese and English when singing, although they fetchingly fail to make much sense in either language. For example: '... I drink tomato juice every night/why don't you get out of my sight ...' is just one line from the song *Tomato Head*.)

During the late '80s *Shonen* ('boy' in Japanese) *Knife* were lauded, and indeed cited, as influences by a number of influential bands, including grunge outfits Sonic Youth and Nirvana. (In 1991, *Shonen Knife* supported Nirvana on a series of live dates, with Kurt Cobain declaring that when he first heard them, he was '... transformed into a hysterical nine-year-old girl at a Beatles' concert'.)

The 2007 album *Fun! fun! fun!* marked the group's 25th anniversary.

KOINOBORI

Every year, on 5 May to be precise, Children's Day is celebrated within Japan. Really, however, it should be called 'Boys' Day', as the numerous *koinobori* or 'carp streamers' that are flown are supposed to install in young males the same sense of courage and persistence that is shown by your average, common-or-garden *koi*.

Now, I just thought that *koi* floated lazily around in some wealthy person's pond until such time as they got scoffed by a heron (or nicked). But apparently not – in the wild, they are, in fact, hardy little buggers that have a tendency to battle their way upstream.

Incidentally, the ancient Chinese believed that *koi* eventually swam all the way up to heaven where they were transformed into dragons. I think it far more likely that, by hook or by crook, that old heron finally got 'em.

KUMADE

Literally 'bear-hand', though here the word 'claw' is probably more apposite. A rake, basically, that is still considered by some to be a good-luck charm. Why? Because an old Japanese saying translates as 'Kumade rake in the money'.

So there you have it.

KUIZU MIRIONEA

Or *Quiz Millionaire*, Japan's version of the famous game show that relies more on suspense than it does on speed. The presenter is Mino Monta, who along with Ms Rat-face (*See* **Rat-face, Ms**) seems to be rarely off the television. Monta has a radioactive-looking orange tan and a decidedly frog-like face, which along with his *urusai* ('noisy', 'bossy', 'irritating') attitude makes many Japanese viewers claim to dislike him. Not that any of this keeps him off the box.

His catchphrase on *Kuizu Mirionea* is 'Final answer?', which his contestants confirm by repeating the words in that strange, almost robotic accent many

Japanese adopt when speaking English. And then Monta's froggy visage splits into a frankly scary grin, his eyes bulging as his face moves oh-so-slowly forwards, like a cobra preparing to strike ...

At which point – so long as a reasonably large amount of money is at stake – *Kuizu Mirionea* invariably goes to commercials, allowing Monta to hop back onto the sun-bed for a quick two-minute top-up ...

MA

Not someone's mother, no. *Ma* is actually 'an interval in time or space' that had profound ramifications on what takes place before, after or around it. For example – to give just two examples – *ma* may be a brief moment of silence in a musical performance, or a space left blank in a painting. *Ma* suggests a *something* that is quite often open to interpretation by the listener or viewer, or indeed the actual performer or artist.

Basically 'less is more' – in other words, classic *Zen*.

MAKIWARA

Something *The Karate Kid* probably never used, the *makiwara* (literally 'wood break') was originally created by *karateka* (*karate* practitioners) on the Japanese island of Okinawa.

Commonly a wooden post driven into the ground, slightly flexible and with its top roughly at shoulder-height, it was partly padded with straw and was struck by a *karateka* with his hands, feet, elbows, knees and basically whatever part of his body he thought fit to make contact with.

Makiwara users are easy to spot by their enlarged, calcified knuckles, which enable them to do such things as punch through bricks. The mighty Oyama, in particular, liked to show off by having his minions hit him on the hands with club hammers.

The straw's gone now in favour of leather or plastic, and in a more 'sports-oriented' martial arts environment, many people refrain from using the *makiwara* for fear of developing arthritis.

MANEKI NEKO

The first-time visitor to Japan may well wonder why, in the windows of numerous shops and restaurants – and even in many private residences – there is a large figurine of a cat holding up one paw to the side of its head.

Well, it's representing the Japanese way of beckoning: hand up but palm down, fingers opening and closing. In such a way is it enticing new customers to enter the shops and restaurants, bringing with them (particularly in the case of private homes) good luck. (The higher the paw, by the way, the greater the number of customers or the amount of good luck wanted.)

There exist numerous different types of *Maneki Neko* – the figurines that are black in colour, for example, help to ward off bad luck – and small plastic versions are commonly worn on key-rings as a good-luck charm.

As might be expected, a few legends serve to explain how *Maneki Neko* came to be. One details how, one stormy night, a passing nobleman took shelter under a tree that was near a rundown temple. Looking through the rain, he was surprised to see a cat apparently beckoning to him in the previously described manner.

'Cats don't beckon – get a grip!' the nobleman admonished himself, but still the cat had its paw raised, apparently desiring the man to step away from the tree. This the nobleman duly did, only to watch speechless a few moments later as a bolt of lightning completely destroyed the tree. Naturally, the nobleman followed the cat into the **temple**, where the impoverished priest – old, alone and starving – had long since abandoned any hope of meeting a generous benefactor.

'Hey – how much do you need?' asked the nobleman, opening his purse. 'It's the least I can do, given that your cat just saved my life.'

And thus did everyone live happily ever after.

MANGA

The Japanese for 'comic', *manga* is recognised outside Japan as having a style completely of its own. This is due mainly to the physical characteristics of the (human) characters, all of whom have unnaturally large eyes and frequently gaping mouths.

Of huge popularity within Japan are the *manga* 'anthologies' that crowd the magazine stands, sometimes hundreds of pages long but printed on cheap paper in order to keep costs down. *Manga* is used to depict anything and everything, from stories for preschool children right through to the kind of X-rated magazines that are commonly found in the possession of teenage boys.

Manga artists enjoy a semi-heroic status, largely because the *manga* industry is an incredibly hard taskmaster. Stories abound of *manga* artists scribbling through the night in order to meet an apparently impossible deadline; of collapsing at their desks and being taken to hospital with exhaustion, only to then discharge themselves so that they can do it all over again.

When it comes to overworking – something the Japanese excel at – the *manga* artists are affectionately considered to be in a league of their own.

MANSHUN

Now, if in Japan you meet someone who says that they live in a *manshun* ('mansion'), that doesn't necessarily mean that they've got heaps of money and a twenty-bedroom house.

Originally, *manshun* were very glitzy, designed and built for the upper crust – but they were still just, like, apartments situated within a large building. And they remain so today, toned down in size and design so that the hoi polloi are able to afford them.

Still, it's not everyone who can say they live in a mansion, I suppose, even though it may, in fact, be an apartment that's barely big enough to swing a *Maneki Neko* in.

MEIJI RESTORATION

Right from the moment Commodore Matthew Perry and his **Black Ships** steamed into Uraga Harbour near Edo (now Tokyo), the days of Japan's self-imposed isolation from the rest of the world were numbered.

Also now numbered, by association, were the days of Japan's Tokugawa Shogunate, which had controlled the country for well over 200 years. Finally bowing to the inevitable, the fifteenth Tokugawa Shogun Yoshinobu officially resigned his position in November 1867, stating that '... if ... administrative authority be restored to the imperial court, and ... if the Empire be supported by the efforts of the whole people, then the Empire will be able to maintain its rank and dignity among the nations of the earth – it is, I believe, my highest duty to realise this ideal by giving up entirely my rule over this land ...'

Fine words – but behind the scenes Tokugawa Yoshinobu had been assured that in return for his complicity, he'd continue to wield a certain amount of power and influence in affairs of state.

There seems to have been a degree of dissension even in this matter, however, with the more radical leaders of the **Meiji Restoration** being far from happy that Yoshinobu still held some sway over what happened in Japan. These radical leaders wanted the complete surrender of all the former Shogun's territories and a total acknowledgement of the fact that the Tokugawa Shogunate was finished – and following the eighteen-month-long 'War of the Restoration' against forces loyal to Yoshinobu, that's exactly what they got.

In Tokyo (formerly Edo), the teenage Emperor Meiji was restored to power, and all that was deemed good about the West – from fashion and diet (beef, for example, suddenly became much more popular) right through to the Industrial Revolution – rapidly began transforming this formerly isolated and feudalistic island country.

As is so often the case, however, very little really changed at the top of the tree. The Emperor Meiji was a god, explained the leaders of the **Meiji Restoration**, directly related to the 'Sun Goddess', and as such was far too important to concern himself with trivial affairs of state. Far better that the leaders of the **Meiji Restoration** should govern on his behalf, as a cliquey and really not very democratic oligarchy.

'How convenient,' muttered the more perceptive of

Japan's populace, some of whom were not really all that enamoured with the change brought about to their country by the Restoration. It rather felt as though it had, ultimately, been forced upon them by the *gaijin*, starting with the visit some years before from the **Black Ship**.

This rumbling discontent would be a long time dying down. Indeed, there are those who would claim that it was still an issue around the time Japan entered the Second World War.

MEISHI

'Oh, yeah – here's my card.'

'Huh? Oh, right, cheers.'

In the West (I'm thinking particularly England), the above dialogue commonly accompanies the giving and receiving of somebody's business card. It can be instantly stuffed into a pocket, or the inside of a wallet, and forgotten. Or maybe, during the course of the meeting, it can be used to scribble a few notes upon – and those sharp corners do make excellent toothpicks.

I think you can guess what I'm going to say now. That's right: it's not the same in Japan. Here, *meishi* are commonly carried around in their own little cases, and there is a definite *kata* to both giving as well as receiving one.

The giving is done right at the start of the meeting or introduction. The *meishi* should be presented using both hands (i.e., thumb and first finger gripping bottom two corners) and with a slight bow or at least a lowering of the head. The *meishi* should appear crisp and fresh, as though it's only just been printed.

The card is received in a similar fashion, and scrutinised by the receiver for at least ten seconds. This, of course, implies that they're taking note of the card details. The receiver then thanks the giver, and bows. If possible, the card remains in front of the receiver (i.e., on top of a desk) for the remainder of the meeting, to be transferred with all due reverence into a wallet or handbag – not a pocket.

Oh, and by the way, never scribble on someone's *meishi*, and never ever use it as a toothpick.

MIFUNE, TOSHIRO

The man who would become the most famous Japanese actor of his generation, was in fact born in China (to Japanese parents) in 1920. Not until he was aged twenty-one did Mifune travel to Japan where, for his pains, he was immediately drafted into the Aerial Photography Unit, where he would remain for the duration of the Second World War.

Following Japan's shattering defeat, Mifune, like so many other young men, drifted, totally unsure of what to do next. Drawing from his wartime experience, he had some vague notion that he would become a photographer – and then, seeing an advertisement for an assistant cameraman at Tokyo's Toho film studio, he applied.

But somewhere there had been a mix-up; instead of being interviewed for said cameraman position, Mifune found himself in front of a panel of judges who wished to assess his acting ability.

'Can you laugh, please?' asked one of the judges.

Mifune's bewilderment at what was happening suddenly turned to anger at this seemingly absurd request. Like many Japanese, he was all but destitute. Starvation was a continual and serious threat. What the hell did he have to laugh about?

The judges felt threatened by the dark look on this young man's tough face. They were about to dismiss him, when one – perhaps a little shrewder than the others – said, 'Okay; act drunk then.'

With a shrug, Mifune decided just to abandon himself to this farcical turn of events. He would never be an actor – but why not give these idiotic men something to talk about later? So, act drunk Mifune did, shouting, stumbling and falling into chairs. Finally he gave up and sat down, glowering at the judges.

Mifune got the job – one of only sixteen men successful out of over 4 000 applicants. And thus began one of the most important periods of Japanese film history. Mifune appeared as a brusque doctor in a near-desolate nineteenth-century village in *Akahige* ('Redbeard'), where in one memorable scene he beats up a number of *yakuza* whose syphilis-plagued brothel he wishes to close down. (Traditionally, many doctors in Japan were little more than glorified bonesetters – and, for some reason often skilled at the martial art of *jujutsu*, they frequently found themselves treating the very fractures and breaks which they themselves had caused. Thus, this scene is not as bizarre as it may first seem.)

1960's *Warui yatsu hodo yoku nemuru* ('The Bad Sleep Well', directed by the masterful Akira Kurosawa) saw a bespectacled, smartly-dressed Mifune seeking revenge from a corrupt industrialist for having caused his father's suicide. And yet Mifune's best-known film in the West undoubtedly remains 1954's *Shichinin Samurai* ('Seven Samurai', again directed by Kurosawa), later reworked into the American cowboy epic, *The Magnificent Seven*. But, regardless of the role played by Mifune – be it a robber, *samurai* warrior, policeman, doctor or fisherman, he brought the same brooding intensity to every film. So well known did his talents become, that George Lucas even considered him for the role of Obi-Wan Kenobi, in 1977's *Star Wars*.

Mifune eventually began to suffer from Alzheimer's, and had become a recluse by the time of his death in 1997.

MINAMATA

A small factory town some 500 miles south-west of Tokyo, Minamata was virtually unheard of to anyone who didn't actually live there. An industrial plant owned by the 'Chisso Corporation' (*chisso* meaning 'nitrogen' in Japanese) that produced drugs, plastics and perfumes, dominated the area and provided employment for many of Minamata's inhabitants. There was also a healthy fishing industry (Minamata being right beside the Shiranui Sea), and thus seafood was the staple diet for most.

Around 1925, the Chisso Corporation began quietly pumping mercury waste from their factory out into the sea – or, to be more precise, into the part that was called Minamata Bay. After a while, the fishermen noticed that they weren't getting anything like as big a catch as before; they looked at the pipes leading from the factory to the sea, put two and two together and complained to the Corporation's directors.

These directors used a mixture of threats and bribes to ensure that the fishermen remained quiet about what they knew – they were paid some trifling sum that was anyway hundreds of times cheaper than the equipment the factory could have bought to render the waste harmless.

Then, in the mid-1950s, some of Minamata's inhabitants began to notice that their pets – particularly their cats, who were commonly fed on fishy scraps – were behaving strangely. They seemed lethargic, unable to walk, their eyes hooded and listless. Many of the town's dogs began to show similar symptoms, and a state of near panic ensued as birds literally began falling out of the sky.

Then it was the humans' turn.

Doctors' surgeries were inundated with people complaining of numbness in various parts of their bodies, extreme fatigue and general nausea. Soon the symptoms of many worsened: convulsions, brain damage, comas. Others became crazy, shouting incoherently.

The ensuing investigation linked the mysterious 'Minamata Disease' to the Chisso Corporation, who discreetly stopped pumping waste into the bay, redirecting their poison into the Minamata River. This flowed right past the town of Hachimon, whose inhabitants – surprise, surprise – were soon exhibiting exactly the same symptoms as those experienced in Minamata.

One investigator – ironically in the employ of the Chisso Corporation – made valiant attempts to get the factory to stop its pollution, be it of the sea or of the river. The response was swift: Dr Hosokawa was hauled into the office, given a severe dressing-down, and ordered to turn over all of his findings for immediate destruction.

The directors also 'paid off' the victims worst affected by the poisoning, while forcing them to sign contracts absolving Chisso Corporation of any blame. A group of fishermen attempted to make a stand, but were soon faced down by a group of thugs called in by the directors.

Only in the late 1960s did the pollution finally stop, and then only because improved production methods no longer made the pumping of mercury waste into the sea necessary. Health officials from outside the area began trying to address the problem of the 3 000-plus victims of the poisoning, some of whom were by now severely mentally and physically disabled.

It would take nearly thirty years for these people and their families to be given proper compensation, although by 2005 over 2000 of these inhabitants of Minamata had died. Today, many of the survivors and their relatives – some poisoned by the mercury waste even as they lay in the womb, thus being born disabled – put on spirited plays and productions for the public, which tell of what happened in the past while at the same providing a warning for the present and future.

MONKEY

'In the worlds before Monkey, primal chaos reigned. Heaven sought order. But the phoenix can fly only when its feathers are grown. The four worlds formed again and yet again, as endless aeons wheeled and passed ...'

And so on. Ahhh ... flashback to the wondrous days of my childhood, when my pals and I would enact this fantastic TV series in the playground. In fact, I do believe 'tis then that my fascination with the Orient began ...

But I digress. *Monkey* was, in the late 1970s, filmed in China and Mongolia with Japanese actors. It was subsequently dubbed into English. It had a completely off-the-wall plot that no-one (at least at my school, but then we weren't the brightest bunch) could even begin to understand. But who cared? It had cloud-surfing nut-cases who were ace at *kung-fu* and who sported amusing names such as 'Pigsy'. And, oh boy, was that *more* than enough.

Subsequent research for this book has unearthed the fact that *Monkey* was based on an ancient – and, at around 100 chapters, somewhat epic – book written in China. It concerned a Buddhist monk's pilgrimage to India, where he has to find some sutras and ...

Ah, whatever. Let's all just whistle, wave our fingers in front of our mouths, and jump on that old cloud for the next nonsensical adventure ...

MONSTER WITH 21 FACES

On the morning of May 10, 1984, a letter arrived at the offices of the Ezaki Glico food company. In it, the group or individual which signed itself off as the 'Monster with 21 Faces' claimed to have poisoned a range of confectionery manufactured by Glico, with potassium cyanide. There was no choice but to recall the products from supermarket shelves – something which cost Glico dearly.

This letter did not, however, mark the beginning of

Glico's troubles. Two months earlier, company president Katsuhisa Ezaki and his family had been kid-
napped, and an unsuccessful attempt made to ransom
them. Then, in April, a number of vehicles in the company car park had been set on fire.

Following the alleged poisoning of Ezaki Glico's
confectionery, the Monster also sent a letter to the
police. Addressing them as '... Dear dumb police officers', it mocked their attempts to find the perpetrator
of the crimes.

Although the Monster stopped targeting Glico, it
then turned its attention to another well-known food
producer, called Morinaga. Two separate incidents
quickly occurred in which Morinaga appeared to agree
to pay a ransom, while secretly arranging with police to
have the 'drop-off' point observed, in the hope of
catching the perpetrator(s). Both times, however, the
ransom payment was not made, while police got frustratingly close to catching someone whom they
described as being a 'fox-eyed man'. (A police superin-
tendent, named Yamamoto, was so distressed at his
self-perceived failure to catch this suspect, that he committed suicide by self-immolation.)

Finally, on August 12, 1985, the Monster sent its last
message – this time to the media. In it, it mocked
Yamamoto's death, and then declared its intention to
'... forget about torturing food-making companies'. But
still police questioned a writer named Manabu
Miyazaki, who made no secret of his links with the

yakuza and who bore a striking resemblance to a composite of the 'fox-eyed man'. Miyazaki was, however, cleared after he provided alibis. To this day, mystery continues to surround the identity of the Monster, with seemingly everyone from right-wing Japanese extremists to North Korean agents being included as suspects.

MR

In Japan, the standard way to politely address/refer to someone is to add *san* at the end of their name. For example, 'Hiro-*san, dozo otabete kudasai.*' ('Hiro-*san*, please eat.') *Sama* is an even politer version, although its use is more limited. (Shop staff may refer to a customer at their store as '*okyaku-sama*' – something along the lines of 'honoured customer'.) Incidentally, you should never use *san* – and certainly not *sama* – when referring to yourself.

Many Japanese are aware that 'Mr' is used in the West as a way of politely addressing a male. They are not so aware, however, that 'Mr' is only ever put before a man's surname. So I often find myself being called '*Mr* Ben' by my *judō* teacher; by the owner of a bar I patronise; and by several of my friends. (The connection here is that such users of 'Mr' speak little or virtually no English. Whereas proficient Japanese speakers of English, of course, often know how to use 'Mr' correctly.)

I secretly find it rather amusing, and thus make no

attempt to 'correct' its erroneous use. And really – unless a *gaijin* male's Japanese is good enough to be able to effectively communicate the reason *why* 'Mr' and a man's first name shouldn't be put together – I believe that this is for the best. I understand that the person using 'Mr' when addressing me is really making an effort to be polite (they could, after all, just stick *san* at the end), and I find that rather touching. After all, who really cares if it's not quite right?

Incidentally, as far as I am aware, *gaijin* women do not receive the same treatment; i.e. having 'Miss', 'Ms' or 'Mrs' stuck before their first name. Regardless of whether or not they are aware of your marital status, the Japanese will simply use *san*.

MUNENORI, YAGYU

So skilled with a *katana* (sword) was Munenori that he became first an instructor and then an advisor to the Tokugawa Shogunate – something which enabled him to earn the somewhat hefty salary of 10 000 *koku* a year. (A *koku* was a measurement of rice approximately equivalent to 150 kilograms.)

Many of the stories concerning his life have clearly been embellished over the years, though it is consistently told of how one day, while meditating in his garden, he was quietly approached from behind by a young assistant. Somehow sensing danger (the assistant later admitted to harbouring a grudge against his master), Munenori jumped to his feet and turned round, at the same time producing his sword. Later – after the assistant had no doubt changed his underwear – Munenori purportedly realised that he'd achieved the swordsman's ultimate goal: that of sensing a danger *before* it even occurred.

MURAKAMI, HARUKI

Probably Japan's best-known modern-day novelist (he has also published a plethora of non-fiction titles), Murakami was born in Kyoto, the son of a Buddhist priest. He currently resides in Tokyo, although he spent four years in the United States during the early nineties. His work has been translated into some forty languages, including Hebrew and Vietnamese. Murakami is heavily influenced by Western culture and music – a fact sometimes discernable just from the titles of his novels. (For example 1987's bestselling *Norwegian Wood*, named after the Beatles' song.) Legend has it that Murakami was inspired to write his first novel (1979's *Hear the Wind Sing*), aged twenty-nine, while watching a baseball game. *Hear the Wind Sing* went on to win him the Gunzou Literature Prize for (as his website describes it) 'budding writers'.

N

NAGAI, TAKASHI

For sheer selflessness and all-round general heroism, Takashi Nagai surely deserves an entry. Born in 1908, and remarkably intelligent from an early age, he worked as a doctor in China before becoming a radiologist at Nagasaki Medical College Hospital. Shortly before the Americans dropped the atomic bomb 'Fat Man' on Nagasaki (August 9, 1945), Nagai diagnosed himself as being terminally ill with chronic myeloid leukaemia – the disease caused by his occupational exposure to radiation. Estimating that he had approximately three years left to live, Nagai vowed only to further devote himself to his work.

But then 'Fat Man' exploded; fortunately, Nagai had already sent his two children to live elsewhere, although his wife was – quite literally – turned to ash as she stood in the family kitchen. Nagai himself was badly injured in the explosion but, ignoring his pain, devoted himself to caring for those other survivors. (While treating the sick and the dying, Nagai – an emaciated figure, covered in bloodstained bandages – would frequently collapse from exhaustion.)

Finally, his considerable mental strength no longer able to override the limitations of his body, Nagai was forced to take to his bed. A shack had been built for him from salvaged materials (his home having been destroyed in the atomic explosion), which Nagai called Nyukodo, which can be approximately translated as 'As yourself hermitage' – the name a reference to the Christian maxim 'Love your neighbour as you love yourself'. (Nagai had long been a convert to Catholicism.)

Still Nagai continued to work, producing an astonishing range of poems, paintings, essays and novels (including *Nagasaki no Kane* – 'The Bells of Nagasaki'; a moving and yet also perceptive account of one of Japan's darkest moments in history). His children had returned to Nagasaki to see him, although his injuries were such that he was unable to have any actual physical contact with them. Wrote Nagai: ... I have to postpone the moment when these children become orphans, even by one day or one hour. Even if it is only one minute or one second I want to reduce the length of time they must suffer loneliness. (From *Kono Ko wo Nokoshite* ['Leaving These Children Behind].)

Finally, on May 1, 1951, at the age of forty-three, Takashi Nagai died. His name continues to live on in

Japan through his writings, and for many he remains an example of how someone can lead a productive life even in the most desperate of circumstances.

NAGINATA

First observed in paintings of battles dating from the 900s, the *naginata* is a weapon rather like the European pike. It was used to best effect against mounted **samurai** cavalry, but was particularly noted for the way it was adopted by a group of people generally not (at that time) considered to be very 'warrior-like'.

I'm talking, of course, about women.

One woman, in particular, the charmingly named Lady Hangaku, proved so adept at using the *naginata* that she ended up commanding around 3 000 soldiers (she probably had something of a strong personality, too). At the very start of the twelfth century, Lady Hangaku and her men fought a fierce battle against an army more than three times their size, with the – apparently exceedingly beautiful – woman's awesome use of the steel-bladed *naginata* causing many a man to fall from his horse, whereupon, unless he got up quickly (and I mean *quickly*), he was dead meat.

In spite of all this, however, Lady Hangaku was captured. Depending on what story you believe, she was then either killed or released to marry a man with whom she had a child.

And so it remains to this very day that *naginata* 'classes' prove extremely popular with women of all ages, although the emphasis is now rather more on *kata* and general *dōjō* etiquette than it is on stabbing a *samurai* in the legs as he sits astride his mighty steed.

NAMBANJIN

If you?re Portuguese and easily offended, it's probably best that you skip this entry ...

Still here? Okay, can't say I didn't warn you ...

For a while in the 1500s, then, the Portuguese were virtually the only *gaijin* to be allowed the privilege of trading with Japan. In particular, the Portuguese and their massive carracks were essential in transporting Japanese silver to China, and Chinese silk to Japan. (Japan and China were, at that time, engaged in one of their periodic spats with one another, which meant they couldn't trade directly.)

As the Portuguese had a reputation for wearing amusing-looking pantaloons and for ... how can I put this delicately? ... not washing very often, they came to be known as *nambanjin* or 'southern barbarians'. They were a source of fascination as well as revulsion to many Japanese, depicted on a variety of fans and folding screens from the time.

Thanks to the Portuguese, and later other foreign traders such as the Dutch, the Japanese were introduced to eyeglasses, 'Western medicine' (which consisted of what, I wonder – a rusty saw, a pair of pliers and a jar of leeches'), and, of course, good old tobacco.

NANSHOKU

Literally 'male colour', and one of the names given to the practice seasoned *samurai* warriors had of taking a youthful male apprentice as a lover. Also referred to as *bidō*, the 'beautiful way', which reflects the fact that this spot of same-sex lovin' was as popular in Japan as it was in ancient Greece.

Indeed, without *nanshoku*, preached one anonymous *samurai* sometime during the sixteenth century, '... it would not be possible for us to maintain the decencies, nor gentleness of speech, nor the refinements of polite behaviour ...'

You old dog, you.

Labelled as something to be ashamed of by Christian missionaries from the fifth century onwards, *nanshoku* had completely fallen from favour by the time of the **Meiji Restoration**, reflecting the less-than-open attitude towards homosexuality within Japan that persists to this day.

NATTŌ

Some time in the late tenth century, so the story goes, a Japanese commander and his men were attacked one day while boiling up some soybeans for their horses. In something of a hurry, then, the soldiers packed up the beans in rice straw, opening the parcel some time later to find that the rice straw bacterium *Bacillus natto* had caused the beans to ferment. (Not that the tenth-century soldiers knew the bit about the *B. natto*.)

'Urgh!' said one soldier. 'That doesn't look too good.'

'If you try eating some,' dared another soldier, 'I'll give you that helmet of mine that you like.'

'What,' said the first soldier ('Taro'), 'the one that's got two massive horns coming out of the top and looks really scary, which makes the enemy wet himself every time he sees it?'

'The very same,' nodded the second soldier ('Jiro').

'You're on,' said Taro, who for the first couple of mouthfuls held his nose while chewing.

'Hey – that's cheating!' said Jiro.

'You know what ...' observed Taro thoughtfully, 'this doesn't actually taste too bad ...'

'Yeah, right!' scoffed Jiro, along with some other soldiers who had by now gathered round to watch.

'No, seriously,' persisted Taro, who really did seem to be enjoying the ghastly looking grub, 'it's dead tasty – far too good for the horses, at any rate.'

'What's going on here?' asked the burly commander, his armour clanking as he walked irritably over to where his men were stood in a large circle.

'It's Taro, sir,' piped up one of the soldiers, at the

same moment describing a circle with one finger by the side of his temple. 'He says that those spoiled soybeans taste nice!'

And he sighed and shook his head, as though to add: *Honestly, I ask you ...*

But if years of military combat had taught the commander one thing, it was never to discount anything as being impossible.

'Give us your chopsticks, Taro,' grunted the commander.

Reluctantly doing as ordered, Taro then watched along with the others as the commander cautiously sampled a mouthful. And then another. And then one more.

'These fermented soybeans are very sticky, and to be honest stink a bit, and are probably what is best described as being "an acquired taste",' observed the commander between thoughtful chews. 'However, I predict that eating *nattō* – which are perhaps best stirred in with rice – will dramatically reduce the risk of heart attacks, strokes, and many different types of cancer.'

Of course, the commander never said that last bit at all. But the benefits purportedly achieved from eating *nattō* now include the reversal of some types of male pattern baldness. This is apparently due to *nattō*'s high concentration of phytoestrogens (whatever they are), which help to lower baldness-inducing testosterone.

Which is great, so long as you can stomach a) the sight, b) the smell and c) the taste of *nattō*.

Personally speaking, I'd rather run the risk of losing my hair.

NEMAWASHI

When transplanting a plant or small tree (for example) from one part of your garden to another, you first make sure to dig around and expose the roots, right? You're preparing the plant for transplantation – it can't just be wrenched from one spot and stuck in another, but instead needs some serious TLC to ease what is otherwise a fairly traumatic process.

Well, that's how it should be in the world of human intercourse, too. By which I mean that people should not be exposed to a sharp, sudden shock, but should instead be allowed to become used to, say, a change of procedure within their company.

This can be done by obtaining their views and opinions before any decision is made, or meeting held. Such views and opinions are given time to bend and adapt to any forthcoming change, thus making a general consensus or agreement that much easier to obtain.

Nemawashi is considered essential in Japanese politics and big business, although a cynic might argue that that's only because it allows for some pretty major corruption. *Nemawashi* is also something that an individualistic *gaijin* can find ever so slightly drawn out and tedious.

NINGEN-SENGEN

On January 1, 1946, millions of Japanese listened to a radio broadcast given by the Emperor Hirohito. For most of those listening, this was the first time that they had ever heard their Emperor speak. And what he said was truly shocking – for in flowery, formal Japanese, Hirohito declared that he was no longer to be considered as some kind of *kami* or 'god' directly descended from the sun-goddess, Amaterasu. His speech became known as the *Ningen-sengen*, or 'Humanity Declaration'.

So what caused Hirohito to say such a thing, along with the instruction that the Japanese were no longer to consider themselves as a race superior to any other? Many historians believe that it was due to a shadowy 'deal' struck between Hirohito and the leader of the US occupational force, General Douglas MacArthur. MacArthur was convinced that Hirohito should remain on the Chrysanthemum Throne and, as such, resisted widespread pressure that he have the Emperor put on trial for alleged war-crimes. (Exactly how much Hirohito knew about Japan's assorted activities during the Second World War has long been a subject of fierce debate. Was he really a somewhat gentle, unassuming man dominated by a military clique? Or was he at least partly aware of the assorted atrocities being carried out in his name')

MacArthur considered allowing Hirohito to remain in his present position an important 'face-saving' exercise for the Japanese people. But, in return for this, Hirohito had to declare that he was not a god, and that his people were not somehow superior to all other races on earth. This Hirohito did; and by the time of his death on January 7, 1989, he had become Japan's longest-reigning Emperor, having sat on the throne for a total of sixty-three years.

NINJA

Here are some things a *ninja couldn't* do:

a. Sneeze.

b. Shout 'Oi, dopey, up here!' at their intended victim from their secret hiding place.

c. Hold down a normal nine-to-five job farming or something, in case they were suddenly called upon to travel the length and breadth of sixteenth-century feudal Japan in pursuit of their quarry.

d. Hang their newly washed uniform outside of their home to dry (a dead giveaway as to why they were commonly out at night).

e. Turn into a wolf or bear (or even a small vole),

make themselves invisible, walk on water, catch arrows with their teeth, climb up sheer rock walls using only their nostrils, disappear in a ball of smoke – unless they inadvertently set fire to themselves – and whatever else you may have seen in various low-budget movies. (I'm assuming here that you have the same discerning viewing habits as myself.)

Here are some things a *ninja could* do:

a. Wait patiently for something to happen without getting bored.

b. Hold onto their bladder, even when they really really needed to go.

c. Scale the odd castle wall during the dead of night, using only their trusty coiled rope and grappling hook.

d. Drop little iron spikes, which really did hurt if you trod on one.

e. Not mind squatting in the pit that was commonly beneath a feudal lord's toilet, knowing that as soon as their target presented his posterior, they could use a sharp stick to ...

Ooooohhhhh ... Bet *that* gave away the *ninja*'s position ...

NOH

If you ever get taken – or even take yourself – to a *Noh* (also spelt *Nō*) performance, be prepared for what could be a slightly long evening ...

No, I'm not suggesting that it's a bit tedious, just ... just something of an acquired taste. As was indeed the intention when it was created by a father- and-son team called, respectively, Kan'ami and Zeami during the thirteenth and fourteenth centuries.

They were both actors, appearing at the vaudeville-like performances that often took place close to a **temple** or shrine. This form of theatre was likely to be attended by both noblemen and the hoi polloi, who if they liked what they saw rewarded the actors with a few coins.

Kan'ami and Zeami were filled with a desire to elevate Japanese theatre from these plebeian trappings, and thanks to the support they obtained from a wealthy shogun called Ashikaga Yoshimitsu (who also had something of a *nanshoku* 'thing' going on with Zeami), they were able to set about doing just that.

'Through the most sophisticated use of language and dance,' declared Kan'ami, 'I want to appeal to the highest strata of Japanese society.'

'Me too,' agreed his son. 'Also, let's get rid of all the tired old plots, sets and over-the-top acrobatics. *Noh* should be more an art form than a performance – in its

Zen-inspired simplicity, it should be the theatrical equivalent of *chado* or the **tea ceremony**.'

What *doesn't* happen on stage, they mused further, is just as important as what *does*. So there should be long, frequent pauses and a general air of slowness to the proceedings. Also, why have a stage cluttered with props and scenery? Surely just a painting of an ancient pine tree on the back wall would suffice.

'Maybe it would be better if many of the actors wore masks,' suggested Zeami. 'All those facial expressions can be very *distracting*.'

'Yes,' nodded his father. 'Emotions can be conveyed just as well by a slight tilt of the head as they can by a facial expression, after all.'

'Maybe not all the actors should wear masks, because that might seem a bit over the top,' said Zeami. 'But certainly even those who don't should keep as frozen an expression as possible.'

Thus began the *Noh* form of Japanese theatre, its Spartan performances and minimal plots often containing a simple message: human beings should strive to free themselves of the trappings of the material world.

Classic *Zen*, in other words.

During the Edo era, *Noh* found itself becoming the 'official performance of the military government' (a great honour, I presume), and even tough feudal chiefs and their battle-hardened men willingly studied something that was considered to be an art form.

However, the inevitable fall from grace came about

after the **Meiji Restoration**. Maybe, as Western influences flooded into the formerly 'closed' island country, *Noh* became slightly too much of an acquired taste, even for many Japanese.

Still it endures, having a small but dedicated bunch of followers. If you see them nodding off during a performance, however, don't think that's because they're bored. In fact, a quick forty winks is almost *encouraged*, as apparently *Noh* is best appreciated while in semi-wakeful consciousness.

Only if 'semi-wakeful consciousness' should happen to you, *do* try not to snore.

O

ODEN

A veritable hotchpotch consisting of such ingredients as boiled eggs, fish cakes, octopus legs, a virtually taste-less gelatinous substance called *konnyaku*, kelp and Japanese radishes which is served in the autumn and winter. (The ingredients are many, and vary from region to region.) Great when accompanied with warm *sake*. For the authentic Japanese dining experience, eat in the evening at a street-side stall.

OMIKUJI

Put your money into the slot (normally ¥100), twist the handle of the dispenser, and out pops your very own *omikuji* – 'sacred lottery'. This will tell you your for-tune, assuming, of course, that you can read Japanese. Congratulations, by the way, if you get *dai-kichi* ('great blessing'), though try not to worry too much if – out of the twelve different type of *omikuji* it's possible to receive – you wind up getting *dai-kyō* ('great curse').

I mean, *I* managed to get *dai-kyō* once – and so to draw the bad luck away from me, I did what you're supposed to do. I tied the scrap of paper to a length of string that was stretched close to the **Shinto** shrine (and there were several hundred already up there, so at least I wasn't alone in my ill-fortune), put my hands together, closed my eyes, lowered my head and looked sincere for a few moments, and then walked stealthily backwards and away.

So far, at least, I've experienced no major calamity ... Touch wood.

ONI

With the best will in the world, *oni* are not what you'd call good-looking. They're humanoid in shape, though they may well have a face like an ape or a bird. Oh, and they might have long fangs and two horns growing out of their forehead, too.

Just in case the above doesn't scare you, they also wear nothing but a loincloth and carry a large wooden club studded with iron spikes. They commonly have names related to the different hues of their skin, such as *akaoni* ('red-demon') and *aooni* ('blue-demon'). I like the putrid-green *oni* best, however.

Oni can commonly be found doing such essential things as guarding the door to hell, though they are often here on earth, too, usually in some remote and mountainous place where they spend their time causing thunder and lightning to happen.

You can sometimes see – particularly on the edge of **temple** roofs – an *onigawara*, which is a *kawara* (tile) moulded in the face of an *oni*. Intended to frighten away other evil spirits, *oni* therefore served much the same purpose as Western gargoyles.

During the spring *setsubun*, people throw heated soybeans out of the doors of their homes, chanting, '*Oni wa soto! Fuku wa uchi!*' ('Demons out! Luck in!')

ONIGIRI

Rice. Wrapped in seaweed. Commonly filled with fish, pickles or *nattō*. A handy snack for ancient **samurai** during those long, gruelling military campaigns, and now a popular convenience food that's sold just about everywhere.

ONODA, HIRŌ

A Japanese commando who for almost thirty years – *thirty years!* – refused to believe that the Second World War was over. Drafted into the military in May 1942, Onoda was trained in guerrilla warfare and, towards the end of 1944, sent to the Philippine island of Lubang, approximately seventy-five miles south-west of Manila.

His orders? To resist any attempt by the enemy (i.e., the Americans) to take the island. However, by the following February Onoda and the small unit he was attached to had failed in their objective – Lubang was firmly under American control.

The Japanese soldiers fought on, determined to at least hamper the American forces, but soon all but four of the guerilla 'army' had been either captured or killed. These four soldiers moved from secret encampment to secret encampment around the island, their diet consisting largely of bananas and iguana meat.

Eventually it all proved too much for Private Yuichi Akatsu. In September 1949 he left the group of four, lasting six months on his own before surrendering to the Philippine army. He was then persuaded (or coerced) into leading groups of soldiers to search for his countrymen, so that the Japanese troops could be persuaded that the war was over.

This effort was a total failure, however, as was an airdrop of letters and photographs (from the hidden soldiers' families, the letters entreating the men to give up) over the island a short while later. The three remaining men were convinced: the war was still on; they had their orders, and any attempt to convince them otherwise was nothing but a ruse. So they would remain in hiding, exercising guerilla warfare, until such time as an invading Japanese force relieved them.

One of the three soldiers, Corporal Shimada, was

shot in the leg by a fisherman in 1953, although due partly to Onoda's medical training he made a full recovery. Less than a year later, however, Shimada was not so fortunate – he was again shot, and instantly killed, when an armed party searching for the hidden soldiers caught sight of him.

Another leaflet drop ensued, and more loudspeaker appeals for the two remaining men to reveal themselves. Onoda's own brother even agreed to come and make an island-wide 'broadcast' – listening from their hidey-hole, however, Onoda and the other remaining soldier, a man named Kozuka, were merely convinced that the voice belonged to a 'sound-a-like'.

So the two men continued to hide out in the forests and mountains of Lubang, taking what supplies they needed from the island's inhabitants at gunpoint. This earned the Japanese soldiers the less than affectionate nickname of 'mountain devils', and ensured that Lubang's farmers and fishermen felt fully justified in taking the odd pot-shot at the two raggedly dressed men whenever such an opportunity presented itself.

In late 1965, Onoda and Kozuka managed to get their hands on a transistor radio, where those few programmes they could understand informed them that Japan was well on its way to becoming a major economic superpower. This (somewhat predictably) they refused to believe – as far as they were concerned Japan was still a nation at war and that was that. They appear, however, to have been somewhat less sceptical about the horseracing reports they were able to pick up – by all accounts they listened to these avidly.

For the following seven years it was business as usual, as Onoda and Kozuka harassed Lubang's indigenous population by doing such things as burning their supplies of rice. But on 19 October, 1972, during one such rice burning, they were surprised by police. The resultant shoot-out left Kozuka dead. Onoda fled back into the forest. He expected to die any day – in fact, he welcomed death as a release to this tormented non-existence, and would have died by his own hand had the orders he'd been given as a commando not expressly forbidden this – and in the ensuing months police, soldiers and ordinary working men alike learned to be wary of sudden sniper fire coming from some heavily wooded area.

Salvation came in the highly unlikely shape of a young university dropout named Norio Suzuki, who'd left Japan with the apparent intention of finding (in no particular order) Hirō Onoda, a panda and the Abominable Snowman.

Suzuki noted that all attempts to locate Onoda had (somewhat obviously) involved the hunters trying to track the hunted. Well, now Suzuki was going to turn the tables. Let Onoda find him. So Suzuki erected his tent within a forest frequented by Onoda, and waited. Finally, his curiosity piqued beyond the point of endurance, the bearded, hollow-eyed and ageing soldier stuck his head through the tent flaps, to see Suzuki sitting cross-legged on his sleeping bag, calmly reading a magazine.

'What's your game, sunshine?' was probably the first question Onoda fired (in Japanese, of course) at the university dropout, before the two men commenced a conversation that lasted several hours.

Two accounts of this initial meeting exist. The first details how the men formed a deep friendship and bond, with Onoda eventually saying something along the lines of, 'Gee, I really have been a bit silly and stubborn, haven't I? There wasn't much point in me living like a hunted animal for the past thirty years, now I come to think about it.'

Far more likely is the account given by Suzuki. In it, the young man details his struggle to make Onoda realise – as one straight-talking Japanese male to another – that the Second World War had in fact ended a very long time ago.

'If ordered to do so by my commanding officer,' Onoda at last declared, 'I'll surrender.'

Undaunted, Suzuki returned to Japan to find this particular commanding officer, who was now quietly earning his living as a bookseller. And in March 1974, Suzuki, Taniguchi and seemingly half the world's press went to Lubang to finally free Onoda of his self-perceived duty. And then Major Taniguchi had to listen patiently for a very, very long time as – with remorseless exactitude – Onoda proceeded to brief him of everything he'd learned concerning the 'enemy' during his near thirty years as a guerilla fighter.

Back in Japan, Onoda was an instant celebrity. His memoirs quickly made him wealthy. And yet Onoda felt as though he didn't even belong in the country that had, in 1959, declared him legally dead. It had changed beyond recognition, the traditional values of the *samurai* replaced by skyscrapers, glitzy technology, and all the other trappings of an essentially decadent society.

So off he went to Brazil to raise cattle, before marriage and an interest in running 'nature camps' for Japanese children finally saw Onoda return to Japan. He continues to be sought by journalists for his views concerning present-day Japanese society and values, and is fond of handing out short, snappy advice along the lines of 'Never complain' and 'Never give up'.

In 1996 he again visited Lubang, to donate $10 000 to a school there and express regret for the more than thirty inhabitants of the island he was estimated to have killed during his near thirty-year guerilla campaign.

ONSEN

Like *sentō* (a public bath), basically, with one important difference: the hot water in the *onsen* comes from a naturally occurring volcanic spring. *Onsen* are sometimes situated near the traditional type of Japanese hotel known as *ryokan*, and have the healing powers commonly attributed to sulphurous-smelling hot water.

Expect either private bathing areas, such as can commonly be found by a *ryokan*, or separated bathing areas according to gender. With regard to the latter, if you're a wee bit modest about such matters I'm afraid that wearing a swimming costume in the communal pool isn't really permitted. Similarly, don't splash around, and when talking, try to keep your voice down.

Oh, and as with the *sentō*, ensure that you use the shower facilities before entering the pool.

ORIGAMI

The ancient art of paper folding. What can you make without the aid of scissors, paper or glue? World Origami Day, by the way, is 24 October, which is presumably when you get to show off that ten-foot-high dragon you've made entirely from sheets of old newspaper.

Be sure to keep an eye out for any smokers, though, especially if they also happen to be slightly jealous *origamika*.

OTEDAMA

Another traditional game, like *kendama*, which Japanese children (particularly girls) used to play in the days before there were such things as PS3s.

Otedama consists – I'll use the present tense here, as in some rare cases you can still see it being played – of some small, cloth bags that are filled with rice, beans or, on occasion, small pebbles. Girls play either together or on their own, singing songs and suchlike as they perform ever more tricky feats of what basically amounts to juggling.

Fascinating to watch, should you ever get the chance.

OYAMA, MASUTATSU 'MAS'

Probably Japan's most famous *karateka* (*karate* practitioner), Oyama was actually born in South Korea in 1923. Then known as Yong-I Choi, he began his martial arts training aged nine, under the tutelage of a man who worked on his father's farm.

Aged fifteen, Oyama decided that he wanted to go to Japan. So off he went; he was what you might call 'headstrong'. Taking his new name in honour of a family who briefly looked after him, he enlisted in the Japanese army with the intention of becoming a fighter pilot.

A premature end to his military career, however, was brought about when he thumped an officer who thought it would be a good idea to bait this gentle-looking young man.

With a lot more time suddenly on his hands (Oyama was fortunate not to be imprisoned for the offence), he started to do some serious *karate* training. And this was real *karate*, by the way, not the sort of glorified 'keep-fit' programme that will get you a black belt in many of today's high-street *dōjō*. Oyama spat blood, broke bones (both his own and other people's) and kept coming back for more.

Then one day, while attending a dance at a local hall, Oyama came to the assistance of a young woman who was being bothered by a drunk.

'Keep out of this!' snarled the drunk (or words to that effect), producing a knife and slashing it wildly in front of him.

With just one blow, Oyama crushed the side of the man's head like an egg. The man fell to the floor, dead. But Oyama hadn't meant to kill, and the fact that he was now a murderer (however justifiable this homicide might have been) devastated him – even more so when he found out that the man's wife and children were facing destitution on a nearby farm.

Completely renouncing *karate*, Oyama went to live and work on the farm for several months by way of penance (the widow appears not to have minded that her husband's killer was helping out).

Finally, absolved of guilt by the dead man's widow, he left and again began training in *karate*. But he soon became bored with practising in the same environment; he needed to train somewhere else – somewhere he would be pushed to the very limits of his endurance, somewhere so harsh it might even destroy him. Basically, Oyama sought an environment that would separate the men from the boys.

'I know,' he decided in a flash of inspiration, 'I'll go and train on top of Mount Minobu in Chiba prefecture. I'll train for around fifteen hours a day, and will take only some books and basic cooking equipment with me. I'll ask a friend to deliver some essential supplies once a week or so – but apart from that, I'll be completely self-sufficient.'

And so it began. From five o'clock each morning, awakening inside a small, chilly cave (probably – it's never actually been said where he slept), Oyama hit trees with his arms, legs and forehead, broke river rocks with his hands, ran up and down the mountainside, practised his *kata* beneath a freezing waterfall, and generally gave himself a very hard time indeed.

'Maybe that's enough,' he thought after eighteen months of such training. So down he came from the mountain, just long enough to win a bunch of *karate* tournaments before deciding that, no, his SAS-like training wasn't yet complete.

Another year passed on top of Mount Chiba, as whoever brought Oyama his supplies each week found themselves beginning to suspect that their friendship was being somewhat trespassed upon.

Oyama himself, meanwhile, decided that as most humans didn't have a hope in hell of standing against him, he might as well have a bash at fighting a bull. What better way to show the world – for such a feat would surely capture widespread attention – that Japanese *karate* was truly a force to be reckoned with?

In fact, Oyama would eventually face over fifty bulls in a bloody showdown between man and beast. He quickly dispatched three of the unfortunate creatures with a straight blow to the head, while depriving most of the others of their horns with his legendary 'knife-hand' strike.

One bull, however, managed to keep its horns long enough to severely gore Oyama. Carted off to hospital, expected not to last the night, Oyama eventually pulled through.

From then until his death, he fought anyone who wanted to fight, while running his own *karate* school. His students were expected to train with almost the same single-minded intensity as himself, which included eight-mile runs bare-chested in winter and brutal 'knockdown' sparring where kicks in the groin were not only allowed but expected.

Not surprisingly, about nine out of ten students said 'Thanks but not thanks' in a high-pitched voice and left to do something rather less demanding, like *ikebana*.

Finally, after a long battle against lung cancer, Oyama passed away on 20 April, 1994, aged seventy-one. His name means 'mountain' in Japanese, and that he surely was.

P

PACHINKO

Do you like deafening noise, blinding illuminations, an atmosphere thick with cigarette smoke and sitting for hours watching small steel balls cascade down the screen of the machine in front of you? If so, then *pachinko* (the name comes from the noise the steel balls make as they rattle about) is for you!

Simply head towards the first cavernous and garishly decorated building you see – usually situated quite close to a train station. It will probably have something really classy like a giant pink illuminated advertisement above its entrance, and large posters of *anime* characters, such as doe-eyed young women with sympathetic expressions and impossibly large breasts that are barely restrained by their skimpy bras.

So put it in your ear-plugs, say goodbye to your lungs, and walk through the sliding doors to where a multitude of (mostly) men sit in front of rows of

machines, using one hand to operate the dial-handle that sends the balls shooting into the machine's 'playing area', while using the other hand to consume an endless diet of coffee and cigarettes.

Such *pachinko* professionals rarely spend less than a few thousand *yen* a time on the trays of steel pulls that are fed into the machines, although individually they cost only around three to four *yen* each. The players are looking for the big payoff, when the balls fall through the pins into one of the scoring slots that pays off with – yep – more steel balls.

Gambling for cash is illegal in Japan, though someone in the *pachinko* world soon figured a way of getting around this minor irritation.

'Why not just be able to swap the accumulated balls – which hopefully now amount to a lot more than you first bought – for prizes such as candy, cigarettes, pens, etcetera?' they pondered.

'You won't get too many customers with "prizes" like that,' observed a friend scornfully. '*Pachinko* by itself is not really that addictive to most people; they need a pretty good incentive to play it.'

'No, these prizes are just a way of getting around the law that prohibits gambling for money,' declared the first person. 'What the player does then is to take their collected cigarettes, pens and so on to what is quite often just a hatch-like aperture down some nearby alley, where a seemingly disembodied hand will reach out to take their prizes, in return providing them with cash. The prizes can later be sold back to the *pachinko* parlour, minus a 'cut' from the people who bought them in the first place.'

'Maybe ...' nodded the friend thoughtfully. 'Seems to me as though all of this is just *asking* for the *yakuza* to take an interest, mind.'

'Well, that's just the nature of these sort of things, isn't it?' uttered the first person philosophically.

It's been suggested that another, less obvious reason for the popularity of *pachinko* is simply that it offers a temporary retreat from Japanese society, with all its strict rules on behaviour and etiquette. In a *pachinko* parlour, a person needn't do anything except stare at their machine and operate the dial-handle, semi-hypnotised by the excessive noise and the many bright lights.

But the main attraction still has to be that with just a few thousand *yen*, it is possible – if you're luck's good, or even if you're just skilful enough to be able to tamper with your machine with the aid of magnet – to earn close to an average month's salary in just a day. Though, of course, some people also lose big, too. As with any form of gambling, *pachinko* has been responsible for a fair few ruined lives over the years.

PARASOLS

Or in Japanese, *higasa*. (Literally, 'sun-umbrella'.) It used to be that mainly middle-aged to elderly women protected their skin from all those harmful UV rays with this dainty little item. However, in the last few years younger women have also been getting in on the act (something to which I can personally testify – on a nice sunny day, my wife never leaves home without one). Pale skin is prized by most Japanese women; suntans are not. Dark-coloured *higasa* – black or brown – are the most effective at blocking sunlight, and for the fashion-conscious it is possible to pick up a Ralph Lauren or Burberry parasol at some exorbitant price. Gloves, hats, light scarves and outsized sunglasses may also be worn in a bid to remain pale-skinned and beautiful, although the poor woman can end up looking a bit like the Invisible Man (or Michael Jackson).

PARIS SYNDROME

Japan is famous for being one of the most polite countries on earth. So what happens, therefore, to its people when they travel to another country which perhaps isn't quite so renowned for minding its Ps and Qs? Say, for example, France – and in particular, its capital city.

For just a few Japanese, declared Professor Hiroaki Ota (who coined the term 'Paris Syndrome'), the sudden exposure to the legendary Parisian temper – in the form of a brusque waiter or taxi driver, for example – can prove catastrophic. The Japanese Embassy in Paris subsequently admitted that it receives approximately thirty 'distress' calls a year, and had on several occasions been obliged to find a doctor who could issue a sedative, to allow the Paris-shocked Japanese tourist to be able to get to Charles De Gaulle International Airport and thus back to nice, safe, polite Japan. However, the Embassy was quick to add that, of the approximate one million Japanese who visit Paris each year, the overwhelming majority depart as scheduled and in an entirely tranquil state of mind, taking with them only pleasant memories of their stay.

PORNOGRAPHY

Sex is a serious business in Japan. By which I mean that if you look at the pornography channel on the television set in your hotel room (which I haven't, ever), then you'll observe that: a) the males are very grim-faced, as though they're trying to finish a tax return rather than partaking in the delights of the flesh; and b) that the females adopt facial expressions and make noises which suggest that this whole thing is a painful ordeal that they hope will soon be over. (Which is, quite possibly, not too far from the truth.)

In Japan, genitalia must never be seen on a television screen. Therefore, whenever such a threat arises, that part of the actor's anatomy is instantly pixilated. This can prove incredibly frustrating (apparently), and screwing up your eyes for hours on end in a bid to see 'through' the pixels results only in a blinding headache and a strangely unsettled state of mind (so I've been told).

The porn industry has a long and illustrious history within Japan. Addicts were getting their kicks from saucy wood-block prints many moons before hotel TVs and those bloody pixels were around. These wood-block prints had a somewhat 'come one, come all' theme, featuring as they did men, women, animals, multi-limbed demons, root vegetables and pretty much anything else the artists could conjure up within their sordid little minds.

Leap forward a few hundred years, in fact to the early 1960s, and *Pinku Eiga* or 'Pink Movies' were being shown in Japanese cinemas. Made on an extremely low budget, Pink Movies were rather tame, and certainly showed no – *ahem* – 'working parts'. Tamaki Katori, an actress born in 1938, appeared in what is generally agreed to have been the first Pink Movie – 1962's *The Flesh Market* (classy title) – and, after starring in literally hundreds more such films, proved so popular that she became known as the 'Pink Princess'.

Pink Movies had declined in popularity by the late 1980s – 'AV' (adult videos) and explicit **manga** having sounded their death-knell – but as late as 2007, in an interview with the *Mainichi Shimbun* newspaper, Tamaki Katori declared that she would still – at the age of nearly seventy – perform in *pornography* if '... there was a part for this old girl'. (In which case, thank God for pixels is all I can say.)

PORTABLE ASHTRAYS

Smoke on the move! Portable ashtrays come in a dazzling array of styles and colours, from the discreet black attachment to a *sarariman*'s briefcase to the Union Jack-design closable plastic case, commonly seen hanging from a chain attached to a hip youngster's belt.

As the current advertisement asks (in authentic **Japanese English**), 'Why risk there being not an ashtray at your favourite view place?' It is illustrated with a photo of a young couple having a romantic fag as they survey *Fuji-san* at night.

Smoking retains its lethal allure in Japan. Advertising is still permitted: a brand of cigarette deemed to be 'masculine' features a muscled surfboarder lighting up on the beach; a slim type of menthol cigarette features the face of an attractive young Western woman, along with the caption '*My choice*'.

(What? a cynic might ask. Lung cancer? Emphysema? Or perhaps just plain old heart disease')

Expect to see portable ashtray users in some unlikely places, such as a doctor's surgery (believe me). But along with encouraging lifelong addiction and premature death, the manufactures of the portable ashtray are at least preventing the dropping of cigarette butts in the street.

R

RABU HOTERU

Fancy a quick bit of passion? No, not with *me* ... If you're feeling a bit fruity and happen to have your nearest and dearest close to hand (or even just an obliging friend/acquaintance/random stranger), then you could always try booking into a *rabu hoteru* ('love hotel') for an hour or two.

If discretion is important, never fear – many love hotels have a multitude of entrances, allowing you and your partner to enter and leave separately. There are even covers to put over your car number plate, should you so wish. Just make sure you don't leave anything incriminating on the dashboard or back seat.

Inside, there is commonly a large 'room menu' on the wall. If the photo of a particular room is illuminated, then it's available for hire. Cheaper love hotels tend to have rooms that are actually quite 'hotel-like' – in the conventional way, I mean – though the more expensive ones can boast revolving beds shaped like giant love-hearts and the type of décor that would make Austin Powers blush.

For privacy's sake, the hotel clerk whom you pay (if the transaction isn't conducted entirely through a machine) sits behind darkened or frosted glass. All you really see is a pair of hands; first taking your money, and then passing you the room key.

Many Japanese use love hotels to escape from cramped, often shared accommodation where the walls can quite literally be made from (rice) paper. Teenagers may be looking to get away from their parents, and, indeed, vice versa. Also popular with prostitutes (or 'delivery health workers', as they are euphemistically known) and pornographic filmmakers.

And if all you really, *really* want is a cheap room for the night (boring), then merely arrive after 10 p.m. when the rate for a twelve-hour stay suddenly drops quite dramatically.

RAMEN

A cheap, filling way of eating, *ramen* restaurants (which are often cramped, noisy, steamy places; though none the worse for that) can be found in their thousands all over Japan.

The humble noodle originally made its way over here from China, and comes served with a variety of toppings, which can vary from region to region – sliced pork and chopped green onion, however, would seem to be a bit of a staple.

You'll slurp when eating them, though don't worry about that. In fact, it's expected.

RAP, GRANNY

In 1992, twin sisters Kin ('gold' in Japanese) Narita and Gin ('silver') Kanie celebrated their 100th birthday by releasing their *Granny Rap* single. Although quite honestly rather dreadful, it took the Japanese pop-chart by storm and caused the aged pensioners to become instant celebrities. Welcomed on an assortment of chat and game shows for their beaming smiles and ready wit, they also declared that their long lifespan was due to their '... simplicity of lives and frequent walks'. Kin survived for eight years following their chart success, with Gin dying a year after in April 2001, aged 108. They had been born to a farming family in Nagoya.

RAT-FACE, MS

Ubiquitous television 'personality', instantly recognis-able to anyone who's watched Japanese TV for longer than ten minutes. Ms Rat-face hosts and also appears on a number of game and 'chat' shows that are broad-cast twenty-four hours a day, seven days a week.

Or at least that's how it really, really does feel.

As Ms Rat-face dislikes the camera being on anyone else for more than a few seconds, she employs several cunning techniques to ensure that she is the centre of attention. These include talking, very often and very loudly (her most obvious ploy), and feigning major surprise at the most innocuous of remarks. Take, for example, the following:

Guest: 'Gee, thanks for having me on your show, Ms Rat-face. It's a real pleasure to be here, and ...'

Ms Rat-face: '*EEEEEEEEEEHHHHHHHHHHHH-HHH?????!!!!!*'

Comedians frequently mimic her with the addition of some rodent-like dentures, and, generally speaking, no one seems to be quite sure why she has to be on TV so often.

REBELLION OF THE GRASS

Chichibu in the 1880s, was a mountainous region in the north-west of Tokyo. The peasants who inhabited the area earned a precarious living from raising silkworms. As it wasn't exactly the most steady of occupations, the peasants were often forced to borrow money from local lenders, to be repaid when their crop of raw silk was bought for exportation to the West.

In 1882, however, a global recession caused the price of raw silk to drop dramatically. Already in debt to the moneylenders, the peasants were forced to borrow still more or else face starvation – oh, and just to help matters, the government formed after the **Meiji Restoration** now decided to increase their taxes.

Finally, a man named Inoue Denzo formed *Konmintou* ('The Party') on behalf of the peasants. He, along with other prominent party members, demanded that the government reduce its taxes. He also asked the moneylenders to stop collecting interest repayments for something like a decade – it would take this long, Denzo claimed, for the peasants to get back on their feet again.

Sadly, but not really surprisingly, neither the government nor the moneylenders paid the slightest bit of attention of Denzo's impassioned oratory. Indeed, the moneylenders started to employ evermore brutal ways of extracting the money owed to them by the poor silk farmers.

'Okay,' said Denzo and the other leaders grimly, 'looks like it's time to start meeting fire with fire.'

And so from the ranks of the thousands of repressed and semi-starving peasants, an army was formed.

'We're going to overthrow the government!' came the – somewhat optimistic, it has to be said – battle cry.

'Just don't hurt the common man – and that includes the moneylenders,' pleaded Denzo, as he began to realise just what manner of beast he'd helped to unleash.

Of course, the moneylenders *did* get a very hard time. They were beaten, and had their properties torched to the ground.

The peasant army fared less well against the military force sent by the Meiji government, and with the capture of Denzo and several other ringleaders it was all over.

Denzo, however, ultimately escaped to Hokkaido, where he lived under an assumed identity for over thirty years. Only as he lay on his deathbed in 1918, did he reveal to his family just who he really was.

REVENGE OF THE FORTY-SEVEN RŌNIN, THE

If there is one Japanese legend that sums up the *samurai* spirit of *bushidō* better than any other, it is *The Revenge of the Forty-seven Rōnin*. And, hey, it actually happened. In March or April of 1701, the Shogun Tsunayoshi Tokugawa instructed two *daimyō* (feudal lords) to prepare to receive an envoy sent by the Emperor. As there was a great deal of pomp and ceremony attached to this forthcoming visit, both *daimyō* required extensive training in matters of etiquette.

This was to be provided by an official named (deep breath) Kira Kozuke-no-suke Yoshinaka, who appears to have been a particularly unpleasant individual. Vain and arrogant, he was also in the habit of demanding bribes to do his job properly. He took an instant dislike to one of the *daimyō*, Asano Takumi-no-Kami Naganori. By all accounts, Asano gave Kira as a 'gift' nothing more than some dried fish; and for this perceived insult, Kira needled and mocked the young *daimyō* at every available opportunity, declaring that he was much too unrefined to ever be able to receive the Emperor's envoy.

Finally, provoked beyond endurance, Asano drew his dagger and lunged at Kira. The main injury was to Kira's pride – he otherwise received only some superficial facial injuries – but judgment against Asano was swift and merciless. For his loss of temper, he was ordered by the Shogun to commit *seppuku* – ritual disembowelment. This Asano did; and his land was consequently declared forfeit, his family disgraced, and his servant *samurai* made to become master-less *rōnin*.

Forty-seven of Asano's *samurai* swore revenge against the odious Kira, but they couldn't take any action against the Shogun's official any time soon – paranoid that an attempt would be made on his life, Kira had surrounded himself with guards. The *rōnin* decided that, first of all, they would have to lull Kira into a false sense of security.

So the *rōnin* dispersed, going their separate ways. They knew that they were being observed by spies in Kira's employ; and so they became gardeners, street sellers, even beggars and drunks. On occasion, they were attacked in inns by *samurai* who recognized them and who were disgusted at their apparent failure to avenge the death of their master.

Finally, Asano's former Chief Councillor, Oishi Kura-no-Sake Yoshio, decided that enough time had passed. Kira's paranoia concerning an attempt on his life had by now abated, although his opulent residence remained amply guarded. By means of messages sent secretly, Oishi assembled the other forty-six men, and late in the snowy evening of December 14, 1702, they advanced stealthily upon Kira's home.

It is estimated that Kira had some sixty guards protecting him that evening, all of whom were quickly defeated by the *rōnin*. Meanwhile, realising that the Day of Judgment was at hand, Kira proved his mettle by hiding in a cupboard. He was quickly discovered, then dragged outside and, in the falling snow, offered the chance to commit the noble death of *seppuku*. But he merely whimpered and begged for his life, until finally one of the *rōnin,* in disgust, cut off his head. This the *rōnin* then took to the Sengakuji **temple**, where Asano's tomb was. The *rōnin* placed the head – wrapped in cloth – in front of their former lord's resting place, and prayed for the repose of his soul as they burned incense.

They expected to be arrested for the killing of Kira. Certainly they made no attempt to flee before soldiers sent by the Shogun came for them. And yet, as news about what had taken place spread like wildfire across Japan, public opinion became firmly with the forty-seven men. Had they not, after all, followed the 'code of the *samurai*' to the letter in avenging their master's death? Even the Shogun confessed his admiration of the men's actions, despite the fact that Kira had been one of his important employees.

The forty-seven *rōnin* had to be punished, however. It simply wouldn't do to allow these men who'd pursued their illegal vendetta, to escape punishment. And the law decreed that for such a crime as theirs, the punishment had to be death ...

Finally, the Shogun realised what he could do. The men had to die – and yet the Shogun offered them the chance to commit *seppuku*, which would preserve their honor. Only the youngest *rōnin* was spared (against his own wishes), on account of his age.

So forty-six men killed themselves by ritual disembowelment, and their remains were then placed with great reverence alongside the tomb of their master. Many years later when the man who'd been spared died (of natural causes), he too was interred at Sengakuji temple. Their tombs can be visited to this day.

RIOTS, RICE

From July to September, 1918, large mobs across Japan conducted frequently violent protests against the recent, dramatic rise in the cost of rice. (It had, in fact, virtually doubled in price.) Rice farmers were particularly incensed by the derisory sum being paid for their crop, in comparison to what greedy merchants were consequently charging the public. So a small, peaceful protest conducted in the somewhat remote fishing village of

Uozu, soon escalated into nationwide demonstrations, with police stations, shops and government offices frequently coming under attack. By the end of September, the 'Rice Riots' had led to the resignation of the Prime Minister and his entire cabinet, while some 25 000 people had been arrested for what might loosely be referred to as 'public order offences'.

RYOKAN

A traditional type of Japanese hotel, sometimes situated next to an *onsen*. Tends to feature female staff wearing **kimono**, and will involve you sleeping on a **futon** that's put out for you on the **tatami** while you eat dinner. There are over 50 000 *ryokan* within Japan, leaving the typical holidaymaker who's seeking a bit of 'culture' somewhat spoiled for choice.

RYOTEI

For a long time, the traditional type of Japanese restaurant known as *ryotei* was accessible only to the elite – the movers and shakers in the twin worlds of politics and business. New customers came solely through the express recommendation of an existing patron, who in turn discreetly settled their entertainment 'account' at the end of each month.

The multi-course menu was exotic and fantastically priced, but then this was rather like taking tea at the Ritz – if you had to ask how much something was, you were in the wrong place to begin with. The women who served were usually *geisha*, and could, of course, be trusted never to disclose anything they saw or heard during the course of an evening.

Over the last couple of decades, however, a string of public scandals concerning taxpayers' money being used to subsidise the *sake*-fuelled outings of senior government figures – along with businesses being forced to tighten their belts after the collapse of Japan's 'bubble economy' – have forced many *ryotei* to look beyond their traditional clientele; to open themselves up to the joys of telephone reservations and a credit card at the end of the evening.

But *ryotei* retain a certain degree of snobbery – if you're a tourist hoping to get a feed in one, you're pretty much out of luck, whether you can afford it or not. Most – in fact, for 'most' basically read 'all' – will simply not accept your booking, fobbing you off on some fictional pretext or other.

I've been fortunate enough to eat in a *ryotei* with my wife. We sat at a low table in our own private room, and were brought in numerous dishes consisting of *sushi*, *sashimi*, small fried fish, *tempura* (batter-dipped and deep-fried seafood and vegetables) and a whole dressed crab – and these were only some of the culinary delights on offer – all served on exquisitely decorated china plates.

I subsequently discovered just how much such a meal in such a place would have cost, but on this occasion, thankfully, it was a gift.

S

SAKAMOTO, RYŌMA

Not far from where I live in Nagasaki, on top of a hillside overlooking a cemetery, there is a life-sized metal statue of the man whom (a recent poll discovered) many Japanese most revere after their father.

Ryōma Sakamoto was undoubtedly a braggart and a hothead, but even more so he was a *samurai*, a master swordsman and the type of visionary that Japan so badly needed during the final, unsteady years of the Tokugawa Shogunate.

Born in 1836 to a family who held the rank of 'merchant samurai', Sakamoto took up fencing while still a child. By the time he entered his teens, he was lethal with a blade. He was still in his teens when Commodore Perry and his **Black Ships** landed at Japan's Uraga Harbour in 1853, shortly thereafter forcing Japan to end its self-imposed period of isolation.

This was a source of extreme resentment to many

Japanese, but Sakamoto – along with some like-minded acquaintances – considered that Japan needed to embrace Western technology if it was to develop as a country. First and foremost, therefore, the outdated feudalistic dinosaur that was the governing Tokugawa Shogunate needed to be removed from power.

While helping to establish a naval training base in Kobe (ironically working – in perfect harmony – alongside a member of the Tokugawa Shogunate; a fact that was already starting to cause some serious resentment amongst Sakamoto's followers), Sakamoto tried to convince two different *samurai* clans to set aside their differences and join forces to topple the Tokugawa from power.

At first the two factions refused, citing their long-held hatred of each other and their shared distrust of the young Sakamoto and all his fancy words. Finally, however, the chiefs of each clan agreed that a union between them was the only way in which Japan could hope to move forward out of the feudal dark age. Sakamoto had successfully brokered a partnership – a joining together of two entirely different forces – that many had considered impossible.

Of course, the Tokugawa Shogunate had their eyes and ears everywhere, meaning that they soon found out just what Sakamoto was up to. To say that they weren't entirely happy is something of an understatement; in fact, they arranged to have Sakamoto assassinated.

Maybe they should have used the traditional *ninja* instead of a couple of heavy-footed agents, because (staying at that time in an inn) Sakamoto was sufficiently forewarned of their presence to be able to defend himself with a revolver and make good his escape.

By all accounts the *samurai* was a fatalist, well aware that his time on this earth would be brief. But before his life ended, he was determined to see the end of the Tokugawa Shogunate.

The two *samurai* clans Sakamoto had succeeded in uniting, along with many of the young man's followers, were champing at the bit in anticipation of a military campaign against the Tokugawa Shogunate. So they reacted angrily when Sakamoto suddenly seemed to switch his thinking, explaining that the Tokugawa could be persuaded to relinquish power if they were made to realise the hopelessness of their position. In such a way, said Sakamoto, could a bloody civil war be averted.

For this, I think, Sakamoto should have been congratulated – even more so when things did go exactly according to plan. The fifteenth Tokugawa Shogun Yoshinobu officially resigned his position, the Emperor Meiji was put on the throne in the newly named Tokyo (formerly Edo), a government (though in truth more like an oligarchy) was established, and although some Tokugawa diehards forced an eighteen-month 'War of the Restoration', this did not involve the average citizen and was in general fought in areas of Japan that were quite remote and sparsely populated.

But although Sakamoto – in light of his predication of an early demise – lived to see the abdication of the feudal shogun, he did not survive long enough to see out the **Meiji Restoration** in its entirety. At an inn in Kyoto where he'd been hiding out – apparently in full expectation of another attempt on his life – he was surprised and killed by a group of men whose identity remains unknown. Either they were *samurai* loyal to the recently disposed shogun, or – as is more likely – they were some of Sakamoto's own men, sick of his popularity and what they perceived to be his habit of going back on his word.

Valiant to the last, Sakamoto's last words are generally reported to have been: 'Oh, look at that, my brains are leaking out of my head ...'

SAKE

Sometimes referred to as 'the drink of the gods', *sake* originally wasn't really a drink at all. Where it first appeared is a subject of some debate (some say China, others Japan), but one thing is clear: *sake*'s been around for a very long time indeed.

But back to my original observation about *sake* not really being a drink at all. Uh-uh – it was, in fact, more like porridge. This was due to the fact that in order to make it, everyone in the village was obliged to chew a mixture of rice, acorns, chestnuts and who knows what else before spitting the wretched mess into a large barrel. This then fermented (a process in which saliva was then essential) to become a sort of low-alcohol porridgy foodstuff.

Hmmm ... make mine half a lager, would you?

Nowadays, of course, we use somewhat more refined methods of production. The quality of the water used in the brewing process is of primary importance, although low-quality *sake* can, and commonly is, served warm to disguise the taste. Otherwise *sake* can be said to be quite like Western wine, with any number of sweet to dry varieties.

Incidentally, when in Japanese company, try to avoid pouring your own *sake*. The person sat nearest you should instead perform this duty, with you doing the same in return.

Anyway – *Kanpai!* (Cheers!)

SAKURA

In the past, the *sakura* – cherry blossom – was closely linked with the life of a **samurai**. It flowered but for a short while, and was renowned for its beauty. (While not denying that the **samurai** lived a dangerous and therefore often shortened life, I think I would, however, stop short of calling them beautiful.)

The *sakura zensen* ('cherry blossom front') begins

around the end of March, starting in southern Kyushu and over a period of about forty days spreading across Japan to ultimately reach Hokkaido.

People gather in local parks and public places to observe the brief, glorious flowering of the *sakura*, to reflect on the fact that the fragile cherry blossom and all it represents vis-à-vis the human condition is still deeply significant to the Japanese character, and also to drink lots of beer and *sake* while generally having a bit of a party.

SAMURAI

The first thing to make clear is that *samurai* were not just mean-looking mothers who were pretty good at hacking off their enemies' heads with their *katana* (swords). Or at least, not necessarily. They could also be quite soulful individuals, fond of composing poetry or plucking the *shamisen* on the occasions when they weren't washing the blood off their armour.

Originally, *samurai* commonly worked on farms in between having a dust-up on some Japanese battlefield. But they were eventually required to choose between one life and the other. If they committed wholly to being a *samurai*, then they were obliged to move into what were known as 'castle towns' – the higher their status as a *samurai*, the closer they lived to the castle (and thus their *daimyō* or lord).

Samurai who lacked a *daimyō* were called *rōnin*. *Rōnin* commonly roamed around Japan, bored out of their skulls and often getting up to all sorts of mischief. They had a nasty habit of producing their *katana* when riled and cutting the source of their annoyance cleanly in half. Generally speaking, when they swaggered into an inn, everyone else walked back out.

The *samurai*'s life was not a particularly enviable one, even when he was in employment. His *daimyō* paid him in *rice* (and you wonder why you never see any pictures of *samurai* smiling'), with which he was expected to keep anything up to twenty staff. This meant that he was usually obliged to go to bed before it got dark, as he could not afford the oil with which to light his room.

In accordance with the codes of conduct inherent in **Bushidō**, the *samurai* was also expected to be entirely without fear and to both expect and welcome death at a moment's notice. In fact, he always wore a short dagger called a *tantō*, should he be required to mete this death out to himself through the ritual cutting of his abdomen called *seppuku*. (*See* **Bushidō** for more information concerning *seppuku*.)

Following the **Meiji Restoration**, the *samurai* had his swords confiscated, and was no longer considered to be Japan's only type of warrior. From then on, a more Western-style army – for example, one that got its manpower through conscription – would be established.

SANGOKUJIN

Or 'third-country-people' – a derogatory term used to refer to residents of Japan's former colonies in China, Taiwan and Korea. During the Second World War, especially, countless men and women from these countries were forced to become slave labourers and 'comfort women' (prostitutes for the Japanese army), both inside and outside of Japan. Before this, in the aftermath of the 1923 Great Kanto Earthquake, thousands of Koreans living in and around Tokyo were attacked by gangs, after false rumours were spread that they were busy poisoning water-wells.

Sangokujin was a term which had all but faded from the Japanese vocabulary, until the infamously right wing Governor of Tokyo, Shintaro Ishihara (*See* **Ishihara, Shintaro**), revived it. During a speech given in April 2000, he declared that – following an emergency, such as another earthquake in Tokyo – *sangokujin* would riot and commit 'atrocious crimes'. Exactly what 'evidence' Ishihara based his typically provocative comments upon, however, remains unclear.

SARARIMAN

Literally 'Salaryman', the much abused foot soldier of economic Japan. Can be observed in their thousands every morning in Tokyo, having endured a hellishly cramped tube journey to the office where they will then routinely work a minimum twelve-hour day.

Finally finishing and breathing a silent sigh of relief as they prepare to go home, they will then acquiesce to their boss's demands and accompany him to a *sunakku* bar where they will be forced to drink to excess and perform endless *karaoke* numbers before eventually being given permission to race for the last train home.

Upon missing said train they will be obliged to pay for an overnight stay at a *kapuseru hoteru*, before waking up the following morning to do it all over again.

SASAKAWA, RYOICHI

'The World's Wealthiest Fascist', as Sasakawa (born 1899) was fond of calling himself, was also commonly referred to as *Kuromaku*. This literally translates as 'black curtain'; the Japanese term for an underworld 'godfather'. (Prior to the advent of electric lighting, *kuromaku* were used to conceal actors in *kabuki* performances while the scenery was changed. The word has also since been used to refer to the general murky goings-on – for example, bribery – that occur within the twin Japanese worlds of politics and business.)

Incarcerated for suspected war crimes by the Americans following the end of the Second World War, Sasakawa was eventually released without charge when the US forces realised just how important his influence could be in ensuring stability within occupied Japan.

While dutifully ensuring that communism was not a

threat to his homeland (he was particularly effective at discouraging any would-be strikers amongst Japan's blue-collar workforce), Sasakawa also set about establishing a gambling empire, though he was just as successful in the field of shipbuilding. A philanthropist, Sasakawa dedicated a great deal of his wealth to charitable causes, in particular working with such organisations as UNICEF to combat AIDS and smallpox within Africa. Sasakawa was also an active supporter of the martial arts within Japan, something which (he declared) ensured that he retained a 'personal army' of unarmed combat experts. (No matter how wealthy and respected Sasakawa became during his lifetime, he never allowed anyone to forget his 'underworld' links, or the fact that he worked alongside the 'establishment' only because he wished to.)

He was truly something of a contradiction: rumoured to have been (in his earlier years) an active figure in the Chinese drug-smuggling industry, and someone who boasted crudely of his sexual conquests of 'over 500 women', he was also an extremely altruistic man, who genuinely cared for the impoverished in Third World nations. His 'Sasakawa Foundation' (which continues to this day as the 'Nippon Foundation') sported the slogan 'Together to Tomorrow', and three years before his death on July 18, 1995, he was honoured by the US Senate as having been '... instrumental in many global efforts to promote a better life for all the world's people'.

SASHIMI

Yep, that fish in the centre of the dinner table sure does look good, neatly sliced and garnished with such delights as shredded radish. If you can get over the fact that it's raw (and a lot of *gaijin* still can't, stubborn devils), then just dive straight in with your chopsticks and ...

Hang on ... Did I just see ... – That fish is ... *moving* ... It's still alive!

Animal lovers beware: to ensure 'freshness', the unfortunate fish is often sliced and diced while still breathing. Some people will no doubt claim that the fish 'doesn't feel a thing', while others will argue that being cut into pieces while still alive at least looks just a little bit painful.

Of course, most *sashimi* is served in portions that do not include the fish's head and tail. (Don't look at the fish's mouth if you're easily upset: that slow, mournful 'opening-and-closing' really can be quite distressing.) Dip the thin slices in *shoyu*, and eat accompanied with *sake* or a nice cold Kirin lager.

SCOOTERS

While in Japan, give yourself a point every time you see one of the following (this game can be played with friends, to add a little competition to the proceedings):

a. The 'James Dean' of the Japanese scooter-world, who revs his under-powered hog while wearing a black helmet that could only ever have got that scuffed and battered with a little assistance from some sandpaper and a small hammer. Expect to see some example of 'biker nihilism' to be displayed on the rider's leather jacket – which, having been translated into Japanese English (*See* **English, Japanese**), may well be virtually incomprehensible. For example: *Sometimes live just lived hard on the road too much*. Give yourself an extra point if James Dean is trying to light a cigarette while at the same time changing lanes.

b. A man and woman in their late teens or early twenties, long hair commonly streaked blond, neither person wearing a crash helmet. As they're young, healthy and good-looking, obviously nothing so trivial as a road accident is ever going to befall them. Give yourself an extra point if the young man (who's invariably the driver) reaches behind him to offer the woman a light for her cigarette, while at the same time trying to turn a corner.

c. A black-robed monk or priest pushing his machine (also usually black) to its very limits as he hurries to a meeting, service or funeral that he's already a couple of minutes late for. Give yourself an extra point if – while waiting at some traffic lights – you see the priest or monk surreptitiously flick his cigarette butt away when he thinks that no one's watching.

d. An immaculately dressed young businesswoman, riding her flawlessly clean machine at exactly fifteen miles an hour, unmindful of the mile-long queue of traffic behind her. Give yourself an extra point if the colour of her helmet matches that of her scooter. Give yourself a million points if you ever once observe her smoking in her entire life.

SE-GA-TAKAI

It is a mystery to me why many Japanese consider themselves to be somewhat dwarfish in comparison to the average *gaijin*. If you're from the West and can boast a few inches on your average Oompa-Loompa, then you instantly stand a good chance of being called *se-ga-takai*, or 'tall'. No matter that this 'compliment' may well come from someone who's not exactly short themselves – in fact may even be taller than you, which has happened to me on several occasions. The Japanese are not – contrary to both their own, as well as popular *gaijin*, belief – short people. I stand a touch under 6ft, and I frequently meet males who are my height or taller. But still this curious Japanese self-denial of their average height persists.

If you're a male *gaijin*, then the description of *se-ga-takai* is also frequently combined with *tsuyoi* – 'strong', or 'powerful'. However, this mixed 'compliment' can best be compared with *jozu* as being not always totally sincere, and may just occasionally cause you to snap: 'I've come to Japan, not effing Lilliput.'

SEIJIN NO HI

On 15 January each year, you may be surprised to see lots of young men and women dressed in either **kimonos** or smart, dark-coloured suits.

Well, on this day they happen to be twenty, and as such are celebrating the fact that they can now smoke, drink and vote to their hearts' content in this 'coming of age' festival.

Tough luck if a person turns twenty even one day after, however – they'll have to wait nigh on another year before they'll be able to celebrate.

SEIZA

The 'correct' way to sit (or rather, kneel) in Japan, particularly during formal occasions and when attending such things as the **tea ceremony**. The Japanese have the ability to kneel for quite literally hours in *seiza*, which is best described as being when the heels nestle under the buttocks. As *seiza* quickly cuts off the blood flow to most Westerners' legs, however, they tend to worry that a double amputation will be necessary, should they remain in the position for anything longer than about ten minutes.

SELF-DEFENCE FORCE, JAPANESE

Article 9 of Japan's 1947 Peace Constitution states: '... The Japanese people forever renounce war as a sovereign right of the nation and the threat or use of force as a means of settling international disputes ...'

Fine words and a commendable attitude – except, of course, for the fact that the Cold War was just around the corner. Suddenly, Japan – 'occupied' by American forces since the end of the Second World War, and set to become a major economic superpower by the mid-1960s – realised that it was worryingly close to some large, Communist countries with whom it did not really have the best of relations. Russia was one, China another – oh, and there was always North Korea, too.

'Our constitution forbids an actual army, per se,' pondered the Japanese, 'and yet nothing's been said about a "self-defence force" ...' So in 1954, two years after the end of the American occupation, a self-defence force is just what Japan permitted itself. The strong pacifist element within the country reacted angrily to this, and yet (countered those in support of the 'force') what would happen in the event of Japan being blockaded by an enemy power, heavily reliant as it was on imported goods? The country would starve, and be brought – once again, when one recalled the terrible days following the end of the Second World War – to its knees.

Far better, therefore, that Japan at least have some way of defending itself should such an event occur. Hence they founded a ground-, air- and maritime-force, which would only act in the case of a specific threat to Japan itself. It could also be used as a relief force, in the event of some disaster occurring within Japan – although when this actually occurred, as in the case of the great 1995 Kobe Earthquake, there was so much red tape to be got through before the self-defence force could be mobilised that a local *yakuza* syndicate proved to be of far more use to the stricken populace.

By the time of the second conflict in the Gulf, Japan's self-defence force had nearly a quarter of a million members and an annual budget exceeding that of the United Kingdom's military. Japan now tinkered with the constitution slightly, allowing for some of its 'self-defence force' to be deployed within Iraq. (They had come in for some international criticism for not having done the same during the 1991 campaign.) Although even in this instance, there were strict limitations on what they were actually allowed to do. They could bear only small arms, for instance, and act as the carriers of supplies, as intelligence gatherers or as medics, rather than engage in any specific fighting.

Which isn't to say that the self-defence force is all bark and no bite, as two North Korean 'shipping vessels' (inside both boats a mass of sophisticated spying equipment – just the sort of thing you need when out fishing for sea bream) found out in March 1999. Challenged and then fired upon by a Japanese destroyer, the two vessels beat a hasty retreat out of Japanese coastal waters.

SENSU

One of the few things that Japan can be said to have introduced to China, rather than vice versa, the *sensu* (a folding fan) was created sometime around the sixth century after someone apparently saw the wings of a bat and was suitably inspired.

Commonly and lavishly decorated with any number of scenes from daily life (the tranquil early-morning calm of a fishing village is a favourite), the number of spindly wooden 'struts' in each fan is said to have been determined by its owner's status in both the royal court and society: so, the more struts you had, the deeper everyone else bowed. (Sixth-century Japanese woman to friend: 'There goes Lady Hinako 'twenty-struts', look. Thinks she's *so* good ...')

Sensu were often (and indeed sometimes still are) used as a way of expressing emotion – both in the **kabuki** and in real life. For a perfect example of this, just picture the **geisha** hiding demurely behind her fan.

SENTŌ

In the days before homes came equipped with their own bath or shower, what did you do when you needed a wash? If you were European and reasonably well off, chances are that you just stuck on a bit more perfume. (Unless you were Queen Elizabeth I, who took a bath as frequently as once a month, 'whether she needed to or not'.)

In Japan, however, people weren't so keen on trying not to breathe when in someone else's company. (You can get used to your own pong quite quickly, apparently.) That's not to say that the Japanese were scrupulously clean by today's Timotei standards, but they still made an effort to attend the *sentō* or public bath reasonably often. Indeed, it was a place where they could relax and exchange gossip with friends while having a good old soak.

And it's mainly for this very same reason that *sentō* survive in many places. As you enter them naked, they're segregated according to gender, and you must make sure – this is really important, by the way – to use the showers first to clean yourself before entering the communal 'pool'. Contaminating the *sentō* with your unwashed body is a major *faux pas*, right up there with entering someone's house without first taking off your shoes, or blowing your nose in public.

(When I first came to Japan, I knew the bit about the shoes. I didn't know about the nose blowing. 'Why do

Japanese men make those disgusting "honking" noises?' I thought innocently, before one day clearing my sinuses into a tissue on a crowded train. *Ooooh* – if looks could kill ...)

SETSUBUN

Don't be alarmed if, sometime around the 3 February (the forth being the first day of spring), you see someone wearing an *oni* mask and being pelted with beans. It's all part of a tradition that dates back to the thirteenth century, as the bean-throwers chant '*Oni wa soto! Fuku wa uchi!*' ('Out with demons, in with good luck!') at the luckless mask-wearer.

For those who are on their own, good luck can be obtained through eating the number of beans that matches one's age.

SHAMISEN

Sometime during the sixteenth century, the *shamisen* arrived in Japan from China. It quickly became the instrument of choice for everyone from *geisha* to the *samurai* – there's even a popular print of a *sumo* having a plaintive pluck – due to its ready availability, cheap price and ease of playing.

Shamisen were then usually covered with the skin of a *hebi* ('snake' – and animal-lovers beware, it gets worse ...), though this didn't allow the three-stringed instrument with the box-like body and long neck to resonate particularly well. The skin of a dog was better, and one canine could commonly cover two *shamisen*, though the best skin for the purpose was that of a cat. Indeed, I have been reliably informed by a **geisha** who played the *shamisen* at a wedding I attended that on the very best *shamisen*, it's possible to see the cat's nipples. Which must surely form the counterpart to the English expression, 'That's the dog's ...'

Maybe not.

SHICHIFUKUJIN

The seven lucky gods. Among them is the god of fishermen (Ebisu), the god of warriors (Bishamonten), and a rather portly fellow called Hotei, whose big belly apparently represents general health and happiness.

Usually depicted riding in a 'treasure ship' (which looks a tad too small for the seven of them – Hotei certainly takes up more than his fair share of room), legend decrees that the gods will reach shore – exactly which shore isn't specified, mind you – along with the New Year, and distribute assorted gifts to those people who deserve them.

SHIKATA-GA-NAI

Much has been said about the famous Oriental – and in this instance, Japanese – ability to put up with misfortune and disaster with no outward display of emotion. Certainly, the Japanese are, as a rule, far less 'demonstrative' than many in the West when they feel that they are being given a raw deal. In fact, it's true that the Japanese will actually often smile when they feel mentally strained, under pressure or otherwise dissatisfied – something which can send entirely the wrong signal to someone unfamiliar with their *bunka* (culture).

(My mother's late godfather, Tony, who for many years did business in Japan, knew this very well. He once did a demonstration for some product to a room full of Tokyo businessmen. His *gaijin* colleague – there for the first time in the Land of the Rising Sun – sat and watched. When it was over, he went over to Tony and said, 'Well, better luck next time.' Puzzled, Tony asked what he meant. 'They all looked distinctly unimpressed,' explained the colleague. 'Just sat there stony-faced with their arms folded.' Tony smiled and shook his head. 'You don't understand,' he said gently. 'When they smile and nod their heads a lot, *then* you've got a problem.' Tony finished this story by saying that a few days later, the seemingly unreceptive businessmen placed a large order for the product – and I wish I could remember what it was – upon which he'd based his presentation.)

Anyway, I've gone off on a bit of a tangent here. *Shikata-ga-nai*, then, can best be translated as 'nothing can be done about it'; something said as a way of getting someone through the most trying of circumstances. In particular, *shikata-ga-nai* is associated with the 1945 – 1952 American occupation of Japan, when countless Japanese stoically tolerated desperate living conditions. But still today, when faced with adversity, many Japanese will utter the phrase at least in their minds.

SHIMABARA REBELLION

Life as a peasant in sixteenth-century feudal Japan wasn't really all that great. You could be knocked about by any *samurai* who saw fit to give you a hard time, and if you wished to remain in one piece you had to pretty much just stand there and take it.

And then there were taxes – the traditional bane of the serf, peasant, feudal slave (call them what you like) since time immemorial. In the case of Japan's feudal underclass, if they also dared to be Christian (a religion largely introduced by the *nambanjin*) then, why, they were just asking for trouble ...

But on 17 December, 1637, some 20 000 over-taxed and God-fearing peasants said something along the lines of 'We're not going to take this' and revolted against their *daimyō* (feudal lord). In the peasants' ranks were also a number of master-less *samurai* or *rōnin*, who no doubt came in handy during the first, bloody encounter with the *daimyō's samurai*.

The peasants won this battle (with the many women in their number proving that they could fight just as hard as the men), although they fared less well against the warriors who were then sent by the ruling Toku- gawa Shogunate. This time, the rebels suffered heavy casualties and were forced to hold up in Hara Fortress, close to Shimabara Castle (situated in present-day Nagasaki prefecture).

The Tokugawa forces set up camp about half a mile away and, using cannons, began bombarding Hara Fortress. Even a Dutch shipping vessel that was lying just offshore got in on the act, asked by the Tokugawa Shogunate to use their guns against the peasants in the interests of retaining 'good relations'.

Surprisingly, none of it did much good. Either they were really bad shots or else the fort was just extremely well made – in any case, the peasants managed to stop yawning long enough to send a message out to the Tokugawa forces.

'Are you so weak that you have to ask a bunch of *gaijin* sailors to help you out?' mocked the rebels, which caused the Tokugawa forces to fly into a dread- ful huff and send the Dutch vessel packing. A classic example of Japanese reverse psychology there, then.

The stalemate between the rebels and the Tokugawa forces lasted for nearly four months, both forces suffer- ing in the grip of an icy winter. However, come March 1638, the rebels were looking at an enemy that had swollen to approximately 200 000 men. There was no way that they could hold out much longer – especially with supplies (including precious gunpowder) now almost totally gone.

Throughout the first half of April, the Tokugawa forces took Hara Fortress bit by bit, continuing to meet fierce resistance that would ultimately cost the lives of over 10 000 of the Shogun's men. The rebels knew that they were fighting for their very lives: they could expect no mercy if captured.

And none were they shown. For the 10 000 Tokugawa warriors killed, nearly 40 000 peasants (this number included many who were loosely labelled as 'sympathisers') were beheaded, with the head of one of the rebellion's main leaders, Amakusa Shiro, stuck on a pole in Nagasaki. There, it proceeded to rot in full view of any other peasants who might otherwise have dared to become dissatisfied with their fairly miserable lot, consequently deciding – perhaps – that another uprising was called for.

SHINKANSEN

Does not, in fact, mean 'bullet train' – that's a Western translation of the Japanese *dangan ressha*, a nickname given to the high-speed project when it was first mooted in the 1930s. The word '*Shinkansen*' actually refers to the **earthquake-** and typhoon-proof train track. (So share this fact at a party, and even total strangers will look upon you with rapt admiration.)

The are several types of train, including the '0 Series' – the front of which does indeed resemble a bullet, hence the famous nickname – but my favourite has to be the '700 Series', with the front cab resembling nothing so much as a duckbilled platypus.

The trains reach speeds of up to 300 kilometres an hour, and on average arrive within six seconds of their scheduled time. (More than sixty seconds and a train is officially classed as late in Japan – as opposed to five minutes in the UK.)

SHINAI

Long ago, when *samurai* were in training for real-life, death-or-glory combat, they tended to use real weaponry, such as swords. Of course, if they weren't very careful they could slice the person pretending to be their opponent (who might, in actual fact, have been a dear and trusted friend) in ways that said dear and trusted friend really didn't want to be sliced.

Eventually, someone pointed out that maiming, or even killing, your *samurai* in training wasn't really such a good idea. Hence the invention of the *shinai*, as used in *kendō* and basically constructed of four bamboo 'staves' tied together with leather and string. The use of the *shinai* thus gave a feeling of authenticity without the risk of any involuntary amputations.

Kendōka (*kendō* practitioners) today carefully inspect their *shinai* both before and after practice to ensure that it is free of splinters and any breaks, although in my humble opinion receiving a bamboo splinter is still preferable to losing an arm – or even worse, your head.

SHINTO

Japan's 'pagan' religion, perhaps as old as time itself, which arose out of man's trembling awe and fear of nature and the world around him. Everything, from the sun and the moon to a spectacular mountain; from a magnificent waterfall right through to a striking rock or tree, was deified as a *kami* (god). Some of the most beautiful *Shinto Jinja* (shrines) are to be found within the woods and forests of Japan, where a stone *torii* (the distinctively oriental-looking 'gateway for the gods') is situated close to the object – be it a rock or a tree with an ornate rope tied around it – that has been enshrined.

Shinto is a remarkably 'easy' religion. It has no particular dogma or prayer rituals, and is more concerned with our lives in this world than with anything that might come after. This is one of the reasons why it exists alongside Buddhism so well: the introduction of Buddhism served to give the Japanese some deeper answers about what might follow death, and reasons as to why they were here on this earth in the first place.

SHIRO

Japanese castles were built for two main and really quite obvious reasons. Firstly, to provide somewhere that a *daimyō* (feudal lord) and his minions could shelter in case of an attack, most commonly from another *daimyō* who quite fancied having a bit more territory. For this reason *shiro* were often constructed on top of a hill or some other natural land elevation, with it being quite usual to divert a nearby (or maybe not so nearby) river in order to supply the necessary moat. And if the *shiro* had a thick forest or cliff-face to one side of it, then so much the better. Anything that would slow down an enemy attack – or force them to come from just the one direction – was considered an asset.

The second reason had nothing to do with warfare and everything to do with vanity. What would a big, flash castle say to anyone who saw it? The obvious conclusion would be drawn that the *daimyō* was doing quite nicely, thank you very much.

Within the castle walls lived the feudal lord, his family and his most trusted servants and *samurai*. And in the town that sometimes lay just outside, the remainder of his subjects, those whom he held most in favour living the closest to the castle walls. (Which meant, of course, that in the event of a surprise enemy attack, when the thatched roofs of the town's huts quickly went up in flames and *samurai* thundered murderously in on horseback, they'd have less distance to run to a place of possible safety – i.e., the castle.)

If there was one thing that let many a castle down, however, it was the frequent use of timber in their construction. Later *daimyō* got a bit smart and started using a lot more stone, but in the beginning *shiro* the length and breadth of Japan were going up in smoke virtually every other week, torched either by enemy forces or just – in the form of lightning – by plain old Mother Nature herself. (With regard to the latter example, remember that many of these wooden tinderboxes were being built on hilltops – all the better to show them off a bit.)

The **Meiji Restoration** and the Second World War saw the destruction of many of Japan's *shiro*, and those that remain today – like Nagasaki's five-storey, white-washed Shimabara Castle, where some fine examples of *samurai* armour can be seen – are often used as museums.

SHISHI

Of the two lion-dogs (*koma-inu*) traditionally stood guard outside a **Shinto** Buddhist shrine, one has its mouth closed while the other has its mouth open. One explanation for this relates to the sound 'ah' – or あ as it is written in Japanese *hiragana*.

あ is the first noise we make upon our introduction to this world – mouth open – while 'un' ('ん as it is in *hiragana*, the final letter of this phonetic alphabet, while あ is the first) is the last sound we make upon leaving it.

Though to my mind it could just as well be 'off', as in 'Yes, of *course* I've turned the power ...'

Just a thought.

SHODŌ

'The way of writing', or calligraphy. Something else that came from China sometime around the sixth century, when it was deemed essential for anyone who belonged to the 'nobility' to practise drawing *kanji* and *kana* characters using a brush and *sumi* (ink).

Within a few hundred years, *shodō* was being practised by everyone, the art being to use brushstrokes of varying heaviness and lightness to express the meaning of what was being drawn. If drawing the *kanji* character 水 *mizu* – 'water'), for example, a *shodō* artist might try to use light, watery strokes to suggest sunlight shimmering off a *kawa* (river) in the late afternoon.

But, of course, once you've drawn a stroke, there's no going back. Just one mistake is one too many, which is why most *shodō* artists seek a pure, almost **Zen**-like frame of mind before committing brush to paper.

SHŌGI

Often called 'the Japanese equivalent of chess'. And the twenty wedge-shaped pieces with which each player

starts the game do have some familiar titles – there's a rook, a king and a bishop amongst others.

The undisputed master of *Shōgi*, Yoshiharu Habu, defines a good player as one who can play an evermore aggressive game – the pace can never start as such only to then become slow and defensive.

Because of this, stalemates are rare – a player's pieces can be 'promoted' upon reaching the other side of the board, and captured pieces brought into play, as (again like Western chess) the players each go after their opponent's king.

SHŌJI

Sliding 'room dividers' or doors that have numerous, pasted screens of *washi* paper (which is sometimes – not always correctly – referred to as 'rice paper') through which the light can filter.

Washi paper is technically stronger than its conventional counterpart, although if you're anything like me you will (if you're not very careful) accidentally stick your fingers through it while trying to open the sliding door. Your Japanese host will, of course, beg of you not to worry, assuring you that the wooden latticework was due to get a new *washi* covering anyway, but you can bet your last *yen* that absolutely none of it's true.

Shōji seem to be coming back into fashion, having in the last few decades been limited to such places as temples and large, 'old-fashioned' residences. *Shōji* are again seen as being an important part of Japanese culture and the traditional *washitsu* (a Japanese-style room, for example covered with **tatami**).

Just watch those clumsy **gaijin** fingers ...

SHŌYU

Soy sauce. Used liberally in Japanese cuisine, although the more health-conscious favour a lighter, lower-salt version since the link between the over-eating of 'traditional' *shōyu* and stomach cancer was first established.

Without *shōyu*, Japanese food such as **sushi** and several meat dishes are all but tasteless. Expect, then, a bowl of *shōyu* to accompany such meals (or a clear plastic sachet if buying **sushi** from a supermarket), in which you can dip said foodstuff.

A quick word of warning – don't leave the *sushi* in the *shōyu* for too long, or else the rice will disintegrate. You're then faced with trying to pick up individual grains with your chopsticks, which ain't easy (trust me).

SONY

It may well today be a $70 billion dollar conglomerate, with its humungous central office based in Tokyo, but Sony began life as a radio repair shop located in what was really little more than a shed. A modest, bespecta-cled gentleman named Masaru Ibuka was the brains behind the outfit, which the following year he called the Tokyo Telecommunications Engineering Corpora-tion.

There was also a co-founder, Akio Morita, who wasn't really all that sure about the name they'd given their company.

'You want something a lot more snappy – something with a bit of, you know, *pzazz*,' he declared.

'Well, what do you suggest?' inquired Ibuka.

'*Sony*,' said Morita.

'I've never heard that word before,' said Ibuka. 'What does it mean?'

'Nothing,' replied Morita. 'That's precisely the point – I made it up. So it's a word that will be entirely *ours*.'

Against his better judgment, Ibuka agreed in 1958 to the name-change. And Sony went from strength to strength. They've weathered a few dud ideas – outside of Japan, for example, their Betamax video system wasn't all that popular, and soon lost to VHS in the 'videotape format war' of the late 1970s/early 1980s – but they struck gold in 1979 with the Walkman (which although virtually the size of a house-brick was still pretty hip for the time), 3.5 inch computer disks, and, in 1994, the PlayStation. And of course, as you're doubtless aware, the company continues to have its many fingers in rather a lot of pies.

SOROBAN

Faster than a calculator? If you get a skilled user then yes, it probably is. Originally coming from the Middle East (first developed, so it's claimed, by ancient traders in Persia), the *soroban* has a rectangular-shaped frame in which there are several thin 'poles', upon which are threaded some small round beads.

I'll come clean here. I haven't got a clue how the *soroban* is used, and despite my mother-in-law's best attempts at teaching me, I remain completely ignorant. Hey, you're talking to someone who got an *F* at GCSE maths. To this day I have trouble deciding – when buying a 500-*yen* item with a 1000-*yen* note – whether or not I've been given the correct change.

However, the *soroban* is generally regarded as being rather difficult to learn – evening classes are usually required – although once you get the hang of it, you'll never look back ...

Apparently. I mean, not that I'd know or anything.

SŌSHIKI

Technically, you can have almost any type of funeral in Japan, according to your religion, although a Buddhist one is by far and away the most usual.

A wake service usually precedes the funeral, held the evening before. The deceased is placed in a deep casket in a special large room or hall within the mortuary, or in front of the *butsudan* (family shrine or alter) if the wake is being held at home.

The casket itself has two hinged 'doors' that are left open above the area of the face. If male, the deceased will be dressed in a suit; females wear a *kimono*. (Occasionally the male also wears a *kimono*, although this is becoming less and less common.)

Mourners bring cash contained in envelopes as a gift, the amount variable depending on how well they knew the deceased. Before the wake begins, the mourners approach the casket and the altar behind it, bow, ring the altar bell, light an incense stick, place it in a pot filled with ashes, and pray. Everyone wears the *juzu* (the Buddhist's beaded bracelet) – on this occasion looped over both thumbs – as they pray.

The mourners extend their condolences to relatives sat close by before going to another, more intimate, room where green tea and coffee are served prior to the actual start of the service. The mourners re-enter the hall upon the arrival of the Buddhist priest, who recites sutras during much of the service. Relatives of the deceased also go up one by one (in order of hierarchy) to the altar and light incense sticks, followed by the other mourners.

When the service is finished, mourners go into the same room where they had tea and coffee before the start. A buffet is commonly served, often consisting of *sushi* and *sashimi*.

Close relatives of the deceased will stay in the same room as the casket overnight.

The funeral itself is usually held in the same room or hall within the mortuary as the wake, although it may also take place at a **temple**. Again, a priest recites sutras, and at the conclusion of the service each mourner may be given a white chrysanthemum (the flower that symbolises death and mourning in Japan) to drop inside the casket, the lid of which has now been removed.

The hearse that carries the casket to the crematorium is a somewhat elaborate vehicle – a sort of mini-**temple** on wheels.

Not much is left of the body following cremation; the bones of the legs and arms mostly turn to dust but somehow most of the ribs remain along with the spinal vertebrae and the skull. You can see all this for yourself as the remains of the deceased are presented on a long metal trolley at the crematorium.

Mourners take it in turns to use a pair of stout wooden chopsticks to transfer pieces of bone into a metal urn, the contents within being periodically crushed by a member of staff in order to make more room. If the deceased was tall, or big-boned, then two urns may be required.

It is always a close relative of the deceased who transfers the Adam's apple or *nodo-botoke* (literally 'Buddha-of-the-throat', so-called because it resembles Buddha seated in meditation) into the urn.

According to Buddhist dogma the deceased now has ahead of them seven different judgements, one taking place every seven days, where it will be decided if they have lied, cheated and committed other unsavoury acts during the course of their life.

If judged innocent of these human sins, they will be permitted entry to Buddha's place of enlightenment.

SPECTOR, DAVE

Without doubt Japan's most popular *gaijin tarento* ('talented *gaijin*'), Dave Spector is a regular on such Japanese programmes as *Tokudane!* (*Scoop!*').

Spector is equally at home interviewing pop stars like Madonna or discussing heavyweight political issues in his rapid-fire Japanese. His tendency to speak his mind about a number of delicate social issues – never afraid to say when he thinks that Japan is in the wrong – makes a refreshing change to some other *gaijin* 'personalities', who, not wishing to rock the boat, ensure that they do little more than grin inanely and generally act 'loveable' whenever they are on television.

During the mid-90s he suffered something of a lull in popularity, due to allegations that he'd 'padded' the qualifications and experience garnered while in his native US (and that's a crime'), but Dave-*san* is nothing if not resilient – as proved by his recent, dramatic escape when the car he was driving suddenly burst into flames – and he soon bounced back.

SPRING OF TRIVIA

Originally broadcast late in the evening, five celebrity judges evaluated assorted nuggets of information sub-mitted on video by viewers, repeatedly pressing a *hē* button when suitably impressed. (*Hē* is a common Japanese exclamation of surprise, commonly inter-preted as 'hey' or 'wow'.)

Since moved to primetime TV, the amount of times the 'hey' button is pressed on *Toribia no izumi* ('*Spring of Trivia*') dictates how much money – in increments of 100 *yen* – the person submitting the item of trivia can expect to receive. (In a typical programme, viewers might be surprised to learn that urine – examined closely – exits the body in a spiral, or that one of Mozart's lesser-known compositions was entitled '*Lick My Arse*'.) The lucky sender of the highest-rated trivia also receives the 'Golden Brain' – a brain-shaped trophy with melon bread inside.

SUMO

The first thing to point out is that these rather portly gentlemen, who wear what bear a remarkable resem-blance to outsized black nappies, are not called 'wrestlers' but *rikishi* ('strong man').

Sumo rikishi are trained in 'stables'. Life for new entrants is made pretty grim; they're up before five to perform the cleaning and so on, and they also have to administer to the wants and needs of the higher-ranking *rikishi*. (And you don't even want to think about what some of these 'wants' and 'needs' actually are ...)

But if the new entrants stick it out and don't quit, as many do, then they too can soon be scoffing great bowls of *chankonabe*, a Japanese stew that takes generously from the animal, fish and vegetable kingdoms. Washed down with as much beer as the *rikishi* care to drink (and when it comes to alcohol, they're not known for being abstemious), it all helps them to pile on the necessary pounds.

When not stuffing their faces or giggling like small girls, *rikishi* practise the art of *sumo*, which basically entails trying to send your partner crashing to the ground, or making him step outside of the *dohyō*. (Despite some fierce protests, by the way, female *rikishi* have yet to be allowed – at least within Japan.)

Many *rikishi* retire when still in their thirties, quitting either while they're still ahead or, contrastingly, when their performance in the *dohyō* has got noticeably worse. It's interesting to note that upon their retirement, *rikishi* often (and quickly) shed a fair few pounds, as in today's health-conscious world it's generally recognised that being so obese commonly carries some adverse side-affects, such as heart failure, strokes and diabetes. There are also other benefits to becoming less vast, but in the interests of good taste we won't go into those here.

SUNAKKU

A bar, basically. Not anything like as expensive as a *hostess bar* but still not cheap. The proprietor is often female and is addressed by her patrons as '*mama-san*'. And that's about it, really. A bar is a bar is a bar, after all.

SUSHI

Raw fish stuck on a bed of rice, right? Well, not always. If the fish is raw, then you can bet your life that it's come from the ocean – tuna, for example. Freshwater fish is never used in *sushi* raw (instead being cooked or smoked), as it has a far greater likelihood of harbouring the sort of nasty little parasites that you don't particularly want to ingest.

The *sushi* chef spends approximately ten years learning his trade; he knows what he's doing and he really does not want to get a reputation for giving his customers food poisoning. So he will also have a good look at whatever ocean fish he intends to use that day. And they'd better have clear eyes, a skin that readily 'bounces back' upon being depressed, and a general lack of a fishy smell, or else they're being pan-fried.

Sushi was originally sold from street-stalls as a sort of cheap, nutritious 'convenience' food, and it remains a staple in many a worker's *obento* or lunchbox. As well as fish, on top of the vinegared rice there can also be meat, egg, mushrooms or vegetables.

A quick word of warning to the unwary: watch out for the *wasabi* – 'Japanese horseradish' – that's usually spread on the underside of the fish before it's put on the 'rice-bed'. It's dyed a light green colour (in cheaper, i.e., non-restaurant *sushi*, it's normally imitation *wasabi*) and it is VERY HOT.

SUZUKI, REVERENT HIROYUKI

During his seventeen-year 'career' as a *yakuza* gangster in Osaka, Hiroyuki Suzuki dealt drugs, gambled, twice went to prison, and was basically that person you don't wish to meet in a dark alley. Arguments with his superiors cost him both of his little fingers (amputated in a traditional *yakuza* form of apology). But in 1990, fleeing from other gangsters to whom he owed a mountain of debt, Suzuki stumbled into a small church in Tokyo and began to transform his life. Soon after, he entered a seminary from where he emerged determined to save others who had nothing but, what he described as, a 'life of lies'. (Some of those helped by Suzuki include a number of his old *yakuza* chums; and in 1992 they carried a large wooden cross across Japan, as a way of advertising their beliefs.) Today he preaches at a small church in Funabashi, east of Tokyo, and has authored a number of books, with such telling titles as *The Tattooed Christian* and *Anyone Can Start Over*. There is also a film based upon Suzuki's experiences, *Jesus Is My Boss*.

SUZUKI, KOJI

Author of the bed-wettingly scary *Ringu* ('Ring') trilogy, which have to date sold in excess of three million copies in Japan alone. A number of Suzuki's books – including, of course, *Ringu* (the highest-grossing Japanese horror film of all time) – have been made into successful movies. Also a popular children's author, he lives in Tokyo, speaks fluent English, and, being the generally talented chap that he is, counts motorcycling and French literature as two of his passions.

T

TAKARAKUJI

Japan's public lottery, which began life some time during the sixteenth century as a way of obtaining sufficient income for the endless maintenance of shrines and temples. It was, however, periodically banned in the years that followed, as various feudal leaders, shoguns, influential Buddhist priests, etc., endlessly debated whether having this lottery was actually any good for the Japanese soul. Revived during the Second World War as a means of financing the war-machine, it continued even after Japan's defeat, with the revenue generated this time being used to help pay for the reconstruction of the shattered country. It is, in the present day, extremely popular – so much so that tickets are often sold on a reservation basis. And much to the lucky winners' delight, all prize money is exempt from income tax.

TAKESHI, KITANO

Commonly known as 'Beat Takeshi', and born in 1947 to a poverty-stricken family in Tokyo. Determined to do better for himself than his alcoholic house-painter father, Takeshi succeeded in securing a place for himself at the prestigious Meiji University in 1965.

Soon, however, he was drawn into Tokyo's 'bohemian' quarter of Shinjuku. For it was within Shinjuku that many of the artists and intellectuals who rebelled against Japan's strict, hierarchal society existed. Takeshi chose to join those who were known as futen – 'mad people' – and ultimately dropped out of university.

Deciding to become a comedian, Takeshi first made a name for himself as part of the duo, 'The Two Beats' (hence his popular title). Their foul-mouthed and politically-incorrect comedy – the disabled and women were frequent targets – quickly proved immensely popular.

Although Takeshi married in 1978, he declared that his wife had drugged him in order to get him to sign the marriage certificate. He also freely boasted of his many affairs, as well as his habit of visiting 'soap houses', where prostitutes perform an erotic cleansing of themselves and their clients before engaging in intercourse.

By the mid-1980s he was presenting *Takeshi's Castle*, an offbeat game show full of physical challenges. He also wrote a number of novels and children's

books – but then, disgusted by the fact that he seemed
to be being almost idolised by the 'Establishment'
whom he held in such contempt, he purposely set out
to disgrace himself, flashing his genitals on live television and beating up staff at a newspaper office. (They'd
published a photo of Takeshi and a woman whom they
claimed was his mistress; on this occasion, curiously,
such an allegation seemed to bother the self-confessed
serial-adulterer.)

Takeshi became determined to 'bury' his comic
career through acting and directing. Typically, the films
in which he appeared were dark and moody, detailing
the nefarious exploits of such characters as hitmen and
yakuza members. At last Takeshi felt that 'his' public
were taking him seriously – but still this failed to dispel
the serious depression which dogged him.

So Takeshi himself has stated that what occurred on
the evening of August 2, 1994 was a suicide attempt.
Takeshi, drunk while in charge of a scooter, crashed
into a road barrier. He suffered serious head and facial
injuries (he'd failed to fasten the chinstrap of his
helmet), and extensive surgery was required on the
right side of his face before he was able to speak again.
But, curiously, the accident seemed almost to 'reinvigo-
rate' Takeshi; although he declared (almost as soon as
he could talk) that he was now drinking 'twice as
much' as before, he had in fact become a much calmer,
quieter and more focused individual. Today, still regu-

larly making and appearing in films, he has become nothing so much as a genuine Japanese icon.

TANUKI

Should you see a creature that looks a bit like Paddington Bear waddling towards you one darkened night, wearing a straw hat and beating its massively oversized testicles like a drum, try not to worry. It's only a *tanuki*, a creature of Japanese myth that can change its shape and which is fond of *sake*, women and song.

Apart from serving as an ad-hoc drum-kit, other uses for the seriously enlarged testes abound. According to the numerous legends that surround the *tanuki*, the testicles have served as everything from a club to a blanket to a parachute (now that's what I call 'well-endowed'). *Tanuki* can even pretend that their scrotal sac is a room, although anyone grinding a cigarette out underfoot isn't too popular to say the least ...

As for the shape-changing bit – one story recounts how, to thank a poor woodsman for saving its life, a *tanuki* turned itself into a traditional looking teakettle, which the impoverished woodsman was able to sell to a priest. Unfortunately for the *tanuki*, the priest then did what you're supposed to do with a kettle, and began to boil water in it.

'Ow!' yelped the *tanuki*, half turning back into its original form as it fled. (From here the story gets even more ridiculous – trapped in its half-kettle/half-*tanuki* form, it returned to the woodsman, and earned a living for the both of them by becoming the world's first half-kettle/half-*tanuki* tightrope artist.)

There is also a *real* creature called the *tanuki* – a fox-like member of the dog family, with stumpy little legs, a bushy tail and a distinctive black line of fur under each eye. They are found in the remoter parts of Japan, as well as Russia, Scandinavia and Europe.

The male *tanuki* also have large testicles, although this is apparently due to their voracious mating habits, and not because they sometimes need their scrotal sac to serve as a parachute.

TAMESHIWARI

The fancy Japanese name given to the habit serious martial artists have of chopping bricks in half, punching through wooden boards, using their foreheads to obliterate a pile of stacked tiles, and so on.

As the disclaimer always says – 'Don't try this at home'. First, you'll need to condition the various parts of your body on something like a *makiwara*, or just wrap a towel a couple of times around a brick and then thump it hundreds of times with the heel of your hand. When you feel ready, just remove the towel.

Speed's very important here – as is belief. Think that you won't break the brick and chances are that your prediction will come true. It'll just be your hand that gives instead. For all the conditioning and all the calluses in the world are a poor substitute for *ki*.

TATAMI

Once upon a time only emperors were permitted to perch their noble behinds upon a single *tatami*, but then various lords got in on the act and eventually it was decided that the mats, which had a woven straw core, reed or rush covering and a decorative edging of cloth, would be quite effective as flooring, being neither too hard nor too soft, but just about right, really.

The average Japanese citizen then had floors of packed earth, until finally – sometime during the 1600 or 1700s – *tatami* became commonplace for everybody.

It's been claimed that they're starting to go out of fashion, but every Japanese home I've ever visited has at least one *washitsu* (a traditionally-styled Japanese room with *tatami*) and often more.

The size of a room is commonly given by the number of *tatami* mats it requires (though the size of the actual *tatami* itself varies from region to region). Incidentally, *tatami* are never set out in a 'grid' pattern – except for sometimes during periods of mourning – as this is thought to bring bad luck.

TAXIS

Are Japanese taxi-drivers the most honest people on earth? Tales abound of them going to considerable lengths – and some personal expense – to return lost property to previous customers.

Indeed, my sister has her own story to tell about this. Dropped off at Nagasaki *eki* (train station) by a taxi, she then proceeded to board a train that was going to Fukuoka, some two hours away. Settling into one of the spacious seats, opening a magazine and awaiting the train's departure, she was surprised to see the same taxi-driver who'd dropped her off at the station board the carriage and advance purposefully towards her.

'But I read that it's not necessary to tip taxi drivers, as a service charge is included in the fare!' thought my sister, as the driver came to a halt beside her seat.

'Your … camera?' he enquired in halting English, holding in front of him the latest, all-singing all-dancing digital wondertoy that had been a present from my sister's partner, and which she'd clearly just left on the back seat of the taxi. You might say that my sister was very grateful. However, she nearly had a companion on her journey, as the driver got off the train just in time – a few moments later the doors shut and off it went.

So excellent is Japan's public transportation system that taxis are more commonly used at night rather than by day, as trains, buses and so on tend to stop running at midnight by the latest. Especially in Tokyo, catching a taxi any time after 11 p.m. can border on being an impossible task.

A taxi's rear left door opens and closes automatically, by the way, and while some taxi drivers speak English and relish the chance to practise it, others, quite frankly, don't.

TEA CEREMONY

Known in Japanese as *sadō* or *chadō*– the 'way of tea'. The practice of drinking tea came to Japan, like so many other things, from China sometime around the ninth century. At first it just seemed like a good idea due to its undoubted health benefits. *Cha* (usually given the honorific prefix *o*) has strong antiseptic properties, and in those days of poor dental hygiene became well known for its ability to stop toothache. It also lowers blood pressure and is packed full of vitamin C (though I don't think they knew about things like that in the 900s), and was generally recognised as being a bit of an all-round vitality restorer.

During the twelfth and thirteenth centuries, the *samurai* began to associate powdered green tea with **Zen** **Buddhism**, where frequent meditation and a simple, austere way of life are encouraged in order that we might gain Enlightenment. But it was one Sen no Rikyū who, in the 1600s, largely developed the complex procedure that is the 'way of tea'. He was the official 'tea-master' (what a great-sounding job title) to the feudal lord Toyotomi Hideyoshi, who rewarded his loyal retainer's years of service by ordering him to commit ritual suicide aged seventy. Which Sen no Rikyū apparently did with quite good grace, muttering something along the lines of 'Oh, the grumpy old goat's having one of his off days, is he?' when he received the bad news from a courtier.

Giving a definitive account of *chadō* from this point on is virtually impossible, as despite the somewhat 'catch-all' translation – i.e., 'way of tea' – many different types of tea ceremonies have evolved over the hundreds of years that have passed since poor old Sen no Rikyū was obliged to end his lifespan somewhat prematurely.

One thing's for sure, though – the tea-host or -hostess will have spent years, possibly even decades, practising their craft. Every superfluous movement made while preparing and serving the tea (and often also a small meal to accompany it), will have been ruthlessly eliminated.

Conversation during the ceremony is kept closely to the matter at hand: the equipment used in *chadō*, which includes whisks, cloths, bowls, the kettle and a bamboo ladle; the sparse appearance of the tea-room, with its **tatami** and hanging scroll; the sunlight that dapples the rice-paper screens of the tea-room's sliding doors and windows (wooden shutters otherwise cover these), or the soft patter of rain outside, the glow of the charcoal fire warming the tea and the soft hiss of the water.

We appreciate all the sights, smells and sounds of the moment – we do not clutter our thoughts and consciousness with anything superfluous. For never again will we experience this time.

TEMPLES

Quite a few of these in Japan, you probably won't be surprised to learn. Some, like the *Kinkaku-ji* or 'Golden Temple' in Kyoto, are truly spectacular, like something out of the Tom Cruise movie *The Last Samurai*. Others, to be honest, look a bit like modern-day office blocks.

You'd like to stay in one (an old-style temple, I mean)? Get away from all those nice, safe, but-oh-so-boring hotels with their polite, smiling, English-speaking staff just for a night or two? Well, why not. Pick up an English-language guide written for any particular area in Japan, and you'll most likely find directions to the local *shukubō* (i.e., a temple that admits paying guests.)

You may also be informed that most *shukubō* work out cheaper than hotels. True. And you might be warned not to expect too many creature comforts – some temples, quite frankly, are not the cleanest of places, which extends to any communal eating areas and washing facilities. (Oh, and get used to the Japanese-style toilet, quick – if nothing else, it's excellent exercise for the thigh muscles.) Also expect curfews, restrictions on smoking and drinking alcohol, a lack of general privacy, and possibly even a demand that you sit in with the temple monks as they recite their evening and morning sutras, which is really quite a novel and interesting experience. For about ten minutes.

Oh, and many *shukubō* request that you book your stay in advance, and are able to speak at least some Japanese (don't assume that there'll be someone at the temple who can speak English, even on a minimum level).

Put it this way: if you turn up at a *shukubō* at ten o'clock at night, just as they're shutting the *mon* (main gate), smiling apologetically and unable to say so much as 'Good evening' in Japanese, you might not get the warmest of welcomes.

If you have no desire to experience any of the above (in my humble opinion it's great to try out once or twice, and is then best left to twenty-year-old backpackers), you can always have a good old nose around the temple 'grounds', most of which are open to the public.

TENGU

Translates as 'heavenly dogs', though there's nothing particularly canine about *tengu*. As every good creature in Japanese mythology should (take as another example *oni*), they live in the remote and mountainous regions of Japan.

In their previous life, a *tengu* was commonly a *samurai* or priest who was particularly arrogant, and who had thus been reincarnated as a red-faced mountain goblin with a particularly long nose. No, I can't really see any connection either.

A *tengu* can take the shape of humans, even a beautiful young woman – but their shadow never changes, and so that hooter really is a dead giveaway to whoever they're trying to fool.

Tengu have no need for shoes, as they vanish from one spot to reappear in another instead of travelling by more conventional means, i.e., walking. They can communicate their thoughts without having to open their mouths (a trick mastered by most teenagers), and if they take a shine to you then they just might teach you their expertise in the martial arts, particularly in the use of the sword (*See Benkei*).

Oh yes – just for a bit of variety, there's also another type of *tengu*. This one has the body of a man but the claws, beak and wings of a bird (bet he's a real hit on the dating circuit). This sort of *tengu* hatches from a great outsized egg that you just might come across if you're out doing a bit of 'rambling' in the wilds of Japan, though for your own sake you'd best not disturb it ...

TENNŌ

Akihito is purportedly the 125th *tennō*, or emperor (*tennō* meaning 'heavenly sovereign') from the semi-mythical Jimmu. It's claimed that the imperial house has managed to maintain a continuous lineage, although many historians and other sceptics would contest that the imperial house is actually being a little less than honest in this matter.

A conclusive answer lies in the imperial tombs, which Japan has traditionally refused to allow open for fear that the spirits of the late emperors might be disturbed. Recently, however, Japan has allowed limited (and I do mean limited) archaeological access to these tombs – though not enough access to scotch the dark rumours that the imperial lineage just might (shock! horror!) have originated in Korea or China.

For centuries the many different *tennō* claimed to be direct descendants of the sun goddess Amaterasu, although Emperor Hirohito renounced this divine status following the end of the Second World War.

TSUNAMI

'Harbour wave', so-called because it's only near to land that this sucker starts to get a bit vicious. Out in the open ocean a tsunami wave may be less than a metre high (although it can be hundreds of miles wide), and so is often unnoticed by the shipping vessels that are riding right on top of it. However, as the depth of the water starts to decrease (i.e., close to land), the wave begins to slow and also put on a serious growth spurt. We're talking an estimated forty metres, when we consider the tsunami waves generated by the eruption of Indonesia's Mount Krakatoa in 1883.

Tsunamis (the word can be pluralised in English, though not in Japanese) are sometimes referred to as 'tidal waves', which is incorrect: as the Krakatoa example demonstrated, tsunamis are not related to the tides. Neither are tsunamis caused wholly by seismic – that is, **earthquake**-related – disturbances: basically anything that can shift a large mass of water – from a landslide or a meteorite right through to a nuclear bomb – can cause a tsunami.

Japan (which of all the countries in the world has endured the most tsunamis throughout the course of history) has spent an absolute fortune on erecting coastal tsunami barriers, although given the height tsunamis can reach just before they hit the shore, the effectiveness of these barriers is at best debatable.

A better bet may be to observe the behaviour of local animals – dogs, cats, rabbits, etcetera. If such animals appear suddenly alarmed, and start to move quickly inland, then the smart money would wager that there's a tsunami a' coming. The animals' behaviour is apparently due to their ability to detect a subsonic 'Rayleigh wave' (and I'd need a degree in physics to even try to explain just what this is), often a couple of hours before the tsunami impacts.

TSURUNEN, MARUTEI

In 2002, after much effort and at the age of sixty-two, Tsurunen succeeded in becoming a member of the Diet (the name of the Japanese parliament in Tokyo). His *meishi* (business card) subsequently declared him to be a 'blue-eyed Dietman', because – here's the kicker – 'Marutei Tsurunen' was actually born Martti Turunen in Finland in 1940. He was, aged four, one of the few survivors of a Soviet attack on his village; and in 1967 he came with his first wife to Japan as a lay Lutheran missionary. Consequently falling in love with the Land of the Rising Sun, and *out* of love with his missus, he got divorced and married a Japanese woman named Sachiko. He taught English, translated some of the epic *The Tale of Genji* (*See* **Genji, The Tale of**) into Finnish and, having written a book succinctly entitled *I Want to Become Japanese,* obtained citizenship of his adopted country in 1979. A growing interest in politics eventually led to him deciding to become a politician, although it would take him around a decade before he was elected to the Diet.

U

UGUISUBARI

Now, just suppose for a moment that you are a feudal lord back in the 1600s. You have a bunch of *samurai* who live close to your castle walls, and of course your own personal bodyguard, but still, sometimes, you are on your own ... Like when you have to sleep in a large, silent and dark castle, which could easily conceal the odd *ninja* (sent, let's say, by another feudal lord) who's creeping silently towards your chamber with murderous intent ... Except for when he suddenly steps on *uguisubari*, specially constructed (via some mysterious technique to do with the flooring nails rubbing against special 'clamps') to chirp like a nightingale when it's trodden upon.

The moment is gone – the element of surprise is lost! Cursing, the *ninja* is forced to beat a hurried retreat from the guards who have been roused from their slumber. He makes it to the window where he got in and scales back down the steep castle wall, all the while lamenting the ingeniousness of sixteenth-century Japanese carpentry.

UKIYO

A 'floating world' that consisted of such delights as tea-houses, brothels, inns and *kabuki* theatres where men – usually governed by strict codes of conduct and behaviour in Edo-era Japan – could for a short while let their hair down, so to speak.

The residents of the *ukiyo* (an ironic reference to the Buddhist belief that this world we inhabit is merely a dream or illusion) – *geisha*, *samurai*, *sumo* and your average Joe looking to get a little action – as well as various scenic spots and famous places, were captured in a series of woodblock prints and paintings called *ukiyo-e*.

UMEBOSHI

Plums pickled in salt and dried by the sun. In days gone by, these served as a virtual meal (along, of course, with the obligatory rice) when there wasn't really much else about.

Rice prevented you from starving to death, at least, although it is – let's face it – hardly the most exciting of foodstuffs. *Umeboshi*, therefore, added a little colour and taste to the proceedings, and remain extremely popular to this day.

If you're a *gaijin*, by the way, eating an *umeboshi* without pulling a face will earn you some major Brownie points.

V

VENDING MACHINES

Let's imagine that it's two o'clock in the morning: the party's still in full swing, when suddenly there's a crisis – there's no more beer! The smokers have run out of cigarettes! What would you do? Maybe a twenty-four-hour garage or convenience store could help out here, if you had one sufficiently nearby (or someone who was sober to drive). But would they stock alcohol, or even allow you to buy it at that time?

In Japan, the solution is easy: just pop along to your nearest vending machine, where you can buy a case of beer or lager (not just individual cans of various sizes) and choose from a wide variety of cigarettes. Which isn't to say that one vending machine sells both beer and tobacco, you understand, though such machines do tend to be found virtually side-by-side.

It's a testament to the general lack of lawlessness within Japan that such machines are virtually never robbed or vandalised – at the very most you might see a spot of graffiti, which generally consists of something like a small '*Herro!*' scribbled discreetly on one side.

Of course, more machines sell soft drinks, iced drinks and general snacks than they do booze and coffin nails. Look out, in particular, for the machines selling 'Boss' coffee and fruit juice produces, which for some reason feature a large photo of a craggy-faced Tommy Lee Jones. (A rather more attractive Meg Ryan is the 'face' of Boss's rival Nescafé in Japan.)

WA

What's *wa?*

Good question. Actually (because frustratingly little in Japan is *ever* 'cut and dried', so to speak), *wa* has lots of meanings. It is, for example, the old Chinese name for the group of 3 000-plus islands that we now know as Japan. It's also used as a prefix to many Japanese words to show that they are, in fact ... umm ... 'Japanese'.

Let me explain: *shoku* on its own, means 'meal' or 'food', but *washoku* means a *Japanese* 'meal' or 'food'. Similarly, *washitsu* means 'Japanese room'. But the meaning we really want for this entry relates to *wa* as a term for 'harmony', 'peace', 'accord' – there can be many different definitions, all of them correct, and yet all of them somehow lacking something.

Like *giri*, part of *wa* relates to the predominant Japanese idea of a person being not an individual, but rather part of a group. Therefore, the needs and wants of the group must always be put above those of the individual, and absolutely nothing must be said or done that alters the status quo.

In other words, here are some things that you absolutely positively don't say (or even think) as part of 'the group':

'I'll put my cards on the table here ...'

'I have to say that ...'

'You'll excuse me for speaking my mind ...'

'Speaking plainly ...'

'It seems to me that ...'

It all relates to the days when rice farming was one of the most common of occupations, and whole villages worked together in the paddy fields to first cultivate and then gather the crop. Any dissension in the group at such times could have had catastrophic results – perhaps even death by starvation, if the villagers refused to pull together – and so *wa* was deemed to be of such importance that it even got a mention in Japan's very first constitution – something along the lines of '... Harmony is to be honoured and maintained ...' And thus it's been ever since.

WABI

Broke, living in dilapidated housing and in dire need of a few friends? Congratulations – you're experiencing the sublime state of *wabi*, or 'beauty in poverty'. Chances are, you're not looking at it that way, though ...

According to **Zen**-Buddhist teachings, only in such a poor, hermit-like state can we truly free ourselves from the meaningless trappings of the outside world (which in this instance could well include cash, central heating and the odd pal with whom to have a drink), thus finding ourselves on the spiritual path to true awakening or Enlightenment. In other words, never pity the poor hermit cause they've actually got things sussed better than you.

Wabi has a companion word: *sabi*, which basically entails finding beauty in things that otherwise might seem just a bit ordinary – perhaps even repellent. Beauty is, at best, a temporary, transient state, so we should not be so fickle as to value this above all else. In other words, a broken old plate is to be valued and appreciated as greatly as a priceless Ming vase.

Apparently. I mean, I know what I'd rather have.

WHALING

Japan claims that it needs to fire explosive harpoons at whales for 'scientific reasons'. And these are? Err ... hang on ... Oh yes: to assess how old they are (or should I say, *were*), what their diet is (generally speaking, I'd guess stuff that you find in the sea), and really important stuff like that.

Greenpeace, the International Whaling Commission, and, indeed, most other countries say that Japan really wants to hunt whales because whale-meat has been considered a delicacy in Japan for well over a thousand years.

Apart from providing a plentiful supply of food, whales also took care of an array of other needs, their oil, bones, teeth and even sinews all having a number of uses, from lighting, right through to the sort of materials that were required for handicrafts. This was, of course, when *kujira* (whales) were plentiful in the world's oceans, and not recognised as being an endangered species by almost every country on earth except for Japan.

But so long as those fancy high-priced restaurants in Tokyo keep needing their meat, the Japanese whaling industry will continue to hunt the noblest animal in the ocean purely out of – ahem – 'scientific reasons'.

WHITE DAY

In Japan, Valentine's Day is observed only by women, who commonly give their partner chocolate. (There is also a custom for women to give men for whom they have no romantic feelings *giri choco*, or 'obligation chocolate'. Again taking place on Valentine's Day, the recipients of *giri choco* may be a woman's work superior and/or co-worker, or someone else to whom she considers she owes a 'debt of obligation'. (*See* **Giri** for a more detailed explanation of this uniquely Japanese concept.)

'White Day' was started – exactly one month after Valentine's Day – so that the male might return the favour (and make the Japanese confectionery industry further large sums of cash). Originally, fluffy white marshmallows were given (hence the name – it was also known at its start as Mashumaro Dei or 'Marsh-mallow Day'), though now gifts such as flowers, hand-bags and shoes are commonly given instead of confectionery.

WOKOU

Throughout the twelfth and thirteenth centuries, Japanese *Wokou* or 'pirates' conducted hit-and-run raids on Korean and Chinese coastal villages, stealing supplies and carting off prisoners to be either sold as slaves or – if they were of some social standing – held for ransom. Finally, in 1419, the famous Korean General Yi Jong Mu led a raid on Japan's Tsushima Island, where many of the *Wokou* were based.

Who emerged victorious in the bloody hand-to-hand fighting which followed, depends largely upon whether one believes the Korean or Japanese account of the battle, written at that time. Though with over 200 islanders slain, and many of their homes and crops put to the flame, it really does seem as though the Koreans came out best. They were able to free those slaves whom they found on the island, and made their defeated foe promise that there would be no more *Wokou* raids. And for over 100 years this promise held true, until the mid-1500s saw those pesky pirates again getting up to their old tricks.

X

XAVIER, FRANCIS

A Jesuit priest who, in 1549, introduced *Kirisutokyo* (Christianity) to Japan. Father Xavier had previously undertaken missionary work in India and Malacca, which was where he met a Japanese gentleman who had the rather striking name of 'Anger'.

'This religion of yours ...' mused Anger one evening. 'I think it might find favour in my own country ...'

Always one to rise to a challenge, Father Xavier landed at Kagoshima a short while later and spent his first year on Japanese soil intensively studying this new and strange language. At last he felt confident enough to start preaching to the natives in their own tongue.

Father Xavier succeeded in making some converts but was then banished from the city by the powers that be, who considered that this *gaijin* priest with his high-falutin new religion was getting a bit too popular. Undeterred, the priest continued preaching around southern Japan, where he helped to found several Christian communities. In total, Father Xavier spent about two and a half years in the Land of the Rising Sun, before setting sail for Goa, leaving his mission in Japan in the hands of another priest.

In Goa, Father Xavier decided to start spreading the gospel through the vast land we now know as China. Before he could put his ambitious plan into action, however, he was taken sick and died.

He left behind, in Japan, a religion that is to this day worshipped by approximately one percent of the population. (A figure that has remained pretty much static from 1549.) Although Christians in Japan have at times endured some pretty draconian measures against them: twenty-six Japanese and foreign Christians were crucified in Nagasaki one freezing day in February 1597 – by order of Taikosama, the slightly nutty ruler of Japan at that time – and Christianity was banned as a foreign religion during the Second World War.

YAKUDOSHI

Are you a) male, and b) twenty-five, forty-two or sixty-one years old? If you are, then you might want to be a bit, umm, well, careful. *Yakudoshi*, you see, are 'calamity years', when you're most likely to suffer a misfortune. (And you women can stop sniggering: nineteen, thirty-three and thirty-seven are all birthdays you've really got no call to celebrate.)

Yakudoshi has, in part, to do with the way the aforementioned numbers sound: Forty-two, for example, can be pronounced *shi-ni*, or 'to death', while thirty-three can be pronounced *san-zan* – 'hard' or 'terrible'. So – just be warned ...

YAKUZA

Technically speaking, *yakuza* means 'useless' or 'good for nothing', though it's best not to remind your average *chinpira* (a low-ranking *yakuza* gangster) of this.

Some *yakuza* would prefer to see themselves less as criminals and more as Robin Hood-type figures, preying only upon the rich and, in times of trouble, helping the ordinary populace. For example, immediately after the great Kobe Earthquake of 17 January, 1995, a local *yakuza* syndicate quickly came to the assistance of those that needed it with food and other essential supplies. Indeed, it was widely noted at the time that the *yakuza*'s response was quicker than that of the government's.

But there's nothing very altruistic about the majority of the *yakuza*'s activities. They're involved in all the usual grey areas of the underworld: extortion, prostitution, debt-collection and worse. Some *yakuza* will buy stock in a large company and then threaten to sit in on the next shareholders' meeting, and perhaps ask a few embarrassing questions about the Managing Director's current marital difficulties, should they not be paid a large amount of money to stay away.

And in any part of a Japanese city that only really comes alive after dark, when young women dressed in 'schoolgirl' or 'cowgirl' outfits stand outside expensive bars and try to entice in passing custom, the *yakuza*'s presence is obvious. They also infest the world of *pachinko*, attracted by the vast sums of money that can pass daily through the *pachinko* parlours. But generally speaking, the average person in the street comes into direct contact with the *yakuza* only in a situation that can best be described as 'unfortunate'.

Take, for example, a young married couple with whom my wife and I are friendly, who were driving home late one night when they were involved in a minor collision with a jet-black gangster mobile. Out jumped the driver – who obviously thought that wearing shades at midnight was a good idea – to demand that the shaken couple reimburse him for the scrape down one side of his car.

'Look at the damage you idiots have caused!' he berated them, although the scrape was clearly weeks old. Besides which, it was the *chinpira* who'd caused the minor accident by jumping a red light in the first place. The next day the couple asked their insurance company to pay up, fearful that they'd otherwise get a knock on their door at midnight.

My wife also remembers the evening when two *yakuza* thugs came to the **temple** where her father was head-priest (a position now held by her brother). Even my wife and her brother, then aged no more than twelve, recognised the men for what they were, due to the previously mentioned swagger and also because one had a somewhat shortened little finger. (When the *Postman Pat* and, later, *Bob the Builder* cartoons were considered for export to Japan, it was planned to add another digit to each of the characters' four-fingered hands to avoid scaring children.

The *yakuza* act of *yubitsume* – 'finger shortening' –

dates from a time when four intact fingers were necessary to get a decent grip of a sword handle. Making someone lop off part or all of their little finger in punishment for some transgression therefore 'weakened' them. Nowadays, however, it's more likely to impede an errant mobster's golf swing.

My late father-in-law invited the two men into his office, where they stayed for about an hour. And most of what passed between them will forever remain a mystery. My wife's father only ever revealed that he informed the pair, politely – as they sipped hot green tea, smoked cigarettes and perhaps nibbled on a cake or two – that they would not be getting any money from him or the **temple**, now or ever. And then the *yakuza* left, never (touch wood) to return.

YASUKE

An African slave, possibly from Mozambique, who was 'presented' to the powerful *daimyō* Oda Nobunaga sometime around 1580. The *Lord Nobunaga Chronicle* – virtually the only source of information we have concerning *Yasuke* – declares that the slave was in his mid-twenties, 6ft 2ins in height (which would have made him an absolute giant amongst the Japanese), and had a strength '... greater than ten men'. He was also '... black like an ox' – something which apparently motivated Nobunaga to have poor *Yasuke* scrubbed, to see if this colour could be removed.

Yasuke (the name 'given' to him in Japan – there is no record of his original) entered into the *daimyō*'s service, and soon learnt to speak Japanese. He may, it's been suggested, even have become a *samurai*.

YONG-SAMA

The Korean actor Bae Yong Joon is more popularly known to his Japanese fans as 'Yong-sama', which can also mean 'royalty' in Japanese. Fame and fortune came Yong-sama's way through the soap opera *Winter Sonata*, which, dubbed into Japanese, duly became a smash hit. His dazzling white smile, boyish good looks, floppy long hair and 'Oh-my-gosh-is-all-this-fuss-over-little-ol'-me?' expression whenever he makes a public appearance, have further endeared him to about eighty percent of the Japanese over-fifty female population.

One Japanese film critic, reviewing the zombie flick *Land of the Dead*, remarked that one particular scene showing a bunch of rather old and decrepit-looking living dead was like '... a get-together of Yong Joon's fan club ...'. And it has to be said that Yong-sama's admirers commonly tend to sport a rather fine purple rinse.

Surely this is not the reason why Yong-sama has recently been hitting the gym, though. And surely his management has had nothing to do with his rather striking change of image, from boyish idol to a muscular man who now doesn't smile quite so often, is 'into' martial arts, and wears his long hair in that peculiar barbarian-style (i.e., with several small ponytails sprouting apparently at random) previously favoured by the likes of David Beckham (*See* **Beckham, David**).

None of the above can be anything like an attempt to attract a somewhat 'younger' fan base, surely.

YOSHIMOTO, 'BANANA'

'Banana Mania' followed the release – at the age of twenty-four – of Yoshimoto's (real name Mahoko Yoshimoto) debut novel, *Kitchen,* in 1988. *Kitchen* went on to sell over six million copies, something which conclusively ended her previous career as a waitress. The daughter of the renowned left-wing philosopher Takaaki Yoshimoto, she attributes her ability to write bestselling fiction to her liberal upbringing, which flew somewhat in the face of traditional Japanese values such as *giri*, and the expectation that a person will – at least partially – repress their own desires and wishes. The young *Yoshimoto* was encouraged to do and think exactly as she pleased; and although her work has often been criticised as verging on being 'chick-lit', much of it still deals with the dreams of the young when juxtaposed with the rigid expectations of Japanese society. For so many of her readers – both within Japan and abroad – *Yoshimoto's* novels are pure escapism.

YOSHITOSHI, TSUKIOKA

Considered to be Japan's last and possibly greatest exponent of *Ukiyo-e* ('pictures of the floating world' –a traditional type of woodblock printing). The unwanted son of a merchant father who'd bought himself *samurai* status, Yoshitoshi (born 1839) was raised by his uncle from the age of three. He demonstrated a genius for *Ukiyo-e* while still in his teens, and much of his work would reflect Japan's turbulent and often bloody transition from being an isolated, feudal-based country governed by the Tokugawa Shogunate, to becoming a land where nearly everything – including its new government – was to some degree influenced by the West.

Although *Yoshitoshi* was interested in – as well as inspired by – the Western art he was consequently exposed to, he paradoxically sought to preserve traditional Japanese culture through his work. Much of what he created was frequently violent (one of his prints, for example, was of a *samurai* committing *seppuku*, while for some reason decapitated women were also often depicted), and bore such succinct titles as *The Sadistic Collection of Blood*.

He became reasonably famous while still a young man; in spite of this, he and his mistress were so impoverished that the mistress felt obliged to become a prostitute so that they might have money with which to buy food. During one particularly cold winter, they were forced to prise up the floorboards of their miserable dwelling and use them as firewood.

What would today probably be diagnosed as clinical depression plagued *Yoshitoshi* all his life; and, having had a succession of lovers, he died alone in the room of a cheap inn, from a cerebral haemorrhage, while still only middle-aged.

Z

ZEN

Zen is everything, and at the same time it is nothing. It is not 'white light' or some divine higher state of consciousness, and yet it can – on its absolute lowest levels – provide the superior state of mind that we require to properly engage in such esoteric pursuits as poetry (for example, *haiku*), painting, *chadō* (*See* **tea ceremony**), *shodō* and the martial arts. In fact, many expert martial artists attribute their feats of *tameshiwari* as a way of 'moving Zen'.

So in this case, what exactly is *Zen*? Surely it must be something, if it can be moved. Well, don't take the word of someone just because they can break five paving slabs using only their little finger (although it's probably a good idea to at least look as though you're taking them seriously). No, we have to find the answer ourselves. Because Zen is indefinable. It exists – if it can be said to 'exist' at all – in a completely rarefied atmosphere, a vacuum. It demands that we free our own mind, absolutely, from all worldly concerns, if we are to stand a chance in infinity of finding it. Allow the mind to learn for itself the very reason for its existence and its capacity for conscious thought – for when you find *Zen*, you will have left the child's toy that is 'conscious thought' a billion miles behind.

Shed yourself of all desire, all wants and needs; an ascetic's lifestyle is not even close to what you'll have to lead if ever you hope to attain *Zen*. There are monks the world over who spend upwards of eight hours a day in seated meditation, their eyes semi-hooded but never closed (because, in all seriousness, closing your eyes does tend to encourage sleep).

Fix your thoughts on nothing; thoughts are nothing but a distraction from *Zen*. Does the goldfish think of anything beyond its immediate, necessary physical functions – to swim, to breathe, to eat? And does it suffer because it has no 'conscious' thought? (I'm not suggesting here that goldfish commonly attain *Zen*-level Enlightenment, by the way. In fact, they probably wouldn't know what *Zen* was if it knocked on their bowl and waved at them.)

Zen has no defining parameters, no shape or form. If ever you think you are close to attaining *Zen*, then you are mistaken, for *Zen* has nothing that can be recognised. Only when you become *Zen* will you truly know it for what it is. Try to grasp it, and away it moves.

Allow the mind and all it contains to dissolve into nothingness – a true nothingness – and you have *Zen*.

Then these words, and the countless millions of others that have been scribbled over the centuries to describe *Zen*, will be rendered of no importance to the real meaning of *Zen* than the scratching of an ant in the earth. For *Zen* can never be described, only experienced.

Which makes the thought of me writing any more seem rather pointless, really.